W9-ACM-269

SCIENTIFIC AMERICAN™

Critical Anthologies on Environment and Climate ™

CRITICAL PERSPECTIVES ON
POLLUTION

Edited by Stephanie Watson

The Rosen Publishing Group, Inc., New York

To my family for their unending support

Published in 2007 by The Rosen Publishing Group, Inc.
29 East 21st Street, New York, NY 10010

The articles in this book first appeared in the pages of *Scientific American*,
as follows: "Atmospheric Dust and Acid Rain" by Lars O. Hedin and Gene
E. Likens, December 1996; "Cleaning Up After War" by Marc Airhart, October
2003; "Everyday Exposure to Toxic Pollutants" by Wayne R. Ott and John
W. Roberts, February 1998; "Can Environmental Estrogens Cause Breast
Cancer?" by Devra Lee Davis and H. Leon Bradlow, October 1995; "Arsenic
Crisis in Bangladesh" by A. Mushtaque R. Chowdhury, August 2004; "Asbestos
Revisited" by James E. Alleman and Brooke T. Mossman, July 1997; "Explaining
Frog Deformities" by Andrew R. Blaustein and Pieter T. J. Johnson, February
2003; "The Oil and the Otter" by Sonya Senkowsky, May 2004; "The Beluga
Whales of the St. Lawrence River" by Pierre Béland, May 1996; "Monitoring
Earth's Vital Signs" by Michael D. King and David D. Herring, April 2000;
"Where the Bodies Lie" by Gary Stix, June 1998; "Questions About a Hydrogen
Economy" by Matthew L. Wald, May 2004; "A Low-Pollution Engine Solution"
by Steven Ashley, June 2001; and in the pages of *Scientific American Presents: The
Oceans* as follows: "Enriching the Sea to Death" by Scott W. Nixon, Fall 1998.

First Edition

Library of Congress Cataloging-in-Publication Data

Critical perspectives on pollution/edited by Stephanie Watson.
    p. cm.—(Scientific American critical anthologies on environment and
climate)
Includes bibliographical references and index.
ISBN 1-4042-0690-6 (library binding)
1. Pollution—Juvenile literature. I. Title: Pollution. II. Watson, Stephanie,
1969– . III. Series.

TD176.C75 2007
363.73—dc22

                                                        2005031026

Manufactured in the United States of America

On the cover: An iron and steel mill in Baotou, China, discharges smoke in
July 2005.

CONTENTS

Introduction

"Pollution" is a word we hear or read almost every day—in the news, in textbooks, and from the mouths of politicians and environmentalists. By now, most of us take for granted the polluted condition of our natural environment. We know that pollution can harm our health, disrupt our environment, and threaten the lives of animal and plant species. We also know that, although pollution can come from natural sources (such as volcanoes), humans are to blame for most of the contamination. It is an unpleasant by-product of the technologies that make our lives easier and our work more productive.

Evidence suggests that our activities have had a direct impact on our environment for thousands of years. The mining and smelting of ore that ushered in the Metal Age (a period from the third to the first millennia BC that included the Copper, Bronze, and Iron ages) sent metallic dust particles into the air and built up potentially toxic wastes, such as mercury and lead. The lead plumbing installed by the ancient Romans poisoned nearly everyone who used it. The

Romans' lead contamination reached as far as Greenland and northern Europe, creating the first long-range effects of pollution. Furthermore, the burning of coal began to deteriorate air quality in England as early as the sixteenth century.

Nevertheless, it is not the ancient but the modern global implications of pollution that most capture our attention. Cars, trucks, and buses choke the highways, spewing carbon dioxide and lead into the air. Power plants burn fossil fuels and emit clouds of carbon dioxide. Factories dump toxic chemicals into our waterways.

We have seen the catastrophic results of pollution many times during the past century, including the following:

- In 1952, the Great Smog killed some 12,000 people in London, England, within a three-month period.
- In 1978, hundreds of residents of Love Canal in New York were forced to leave their homes when some 20,000 tons (18,144 metric tons) of toxic chemicals were discovered buried there.
- In 1984, a Union Carbide gas leak in Bhopal, India, killed nearly 15,000 people and sickened tens of thousands more.
- In 1986, the Chernobyl nuclear power plant exploded and exposed more than 8 million people in the Soviet Union to radiation and

contaminated nearly 60,000 square miles (155,399 square kilometers) of land.

- In 1989, the *Exxon Valdez* tanker ran aground in Prince William Sound and spilled crude oil and coated more than 1,000 miles (1,609 kilometers) of Alaska's once pristine coastline, killing wildlife numbered in the thousands.

These events made headlines around the world. But other potential pollution disasters lurk in the shadows, too gradual and subtle for us to see. Pollutants build up in the environment over a period of many years. They can eventually make their way into the ground, seep into the water supply, and work their way up through the food chain. Aquatic plants growing in waters tainted by toxic chemicals are eaten by small fish. The toxins accumulate in the small fish, which are then eaten by bigger fish or birds. Eventually, the bigger fish can make their way into the supermarkets, where we buy our food.

Pollution leaves its mark on forests, wetlands, rivers, and other ecosystems. These natural resources are essential for maintaining air quality and sustaining a wide variety of wildlife. Gases, such as carbon dioxide, sulfur dioxide, and nitrogen oxides formed from the industrial burning of fossil fuels, come into contact with water in the atmosphere and form acid rain, which contaminates lakes and creates poor growing conditions for forest plants. Sewage, pesticides, and fertilizers are released into rivers and bays, poisoning fish and threatening human health. Billions of tons of garbage and other solid wastes are thrown into landfills each year, contaminating surrounding areas. Hazardous wastes such as toxic chemicals and radioactive substances find their way into the air, water, and soil, contributing to birth defects, cancer, and other illnesses.

Pollution also leaves its mark high above Earth's surface. Hydrocarbons and nitrogen oxides released from cars and power plants react in the presence of sunlight to form ozone, which is harmful to breathe. Past production of chlorine-containing compounds such as chloro-fluorocarbons (CFCs) (which were once used as coolants in refrigerators and air conditioners, as cleaning solvents, and as aerosol propellants) depleted the ozone layer that shields Earth from the sun's harmful ultraviolet radiation.

Scientists are still trying to determine the effects of these pollutants on the environment and on human health. Several scientists have shared the fruits of their research in the articles contained in this anthology. They examine many of the forms of pollution with which we are familiar: acid rain, oil spills, asbestos, and arsenic. But they also challenge our notions of what constitutes pollution. That word may evoke an image of a filthy industrial smokestack spewing noxious chemicals into the sky, but some of the products we use to clean our homes and clothes pose even greater threats to our health. We may think positively of the nutrients that feed our plants, when they are silently starving our aquatic life of oxygen. Conversely, we may think of asbestos only as the highly toxic substance that governments have spent billions to remove from schools and offices, while we ignore its many important uses.

Although this book points out the negative implications of pollution, the news is not all bad. Governments have spent billions to tackle the problem of pollution, and it appears that at least some of their efforts have begun to pay off. In the United States, the Environmental Protection Agency (EPA) was established in 1970 to set and enforce environmental standards. The Clean Air Act (1963) set quality standards for air pollution and reduced certain types of pollution, such as sulfur dioxide emissions. It was amended in 1990 to address modern problems such as acid rain, smog, and ozone depletion. The Safe Drinking Water Act (1974) and Clean Water Act (1977) established higher water quality standards. The Comprehensive Environmental Response, Compensation, and Liability Act (1980), also known as Superfund, addressed the problem of hazardous waste. A 1990 amendment to the Montreal Protocol (1987) banned the production of CFCs by developed countries.

As a result of these initiatives, emissions from cars and power plants have been reduced. Drinking water is safer. Even the ozone layer is showing signs of recovery. Although the effort is far from over, scientists continue to monitor Earth's health and push for new and stricter regulations to protect it. —*SW*

1 Environmental Fallout

It seems like an indisputable rationale: industrial pollutants are bad for the environment, and cleaning them up will make the environment safer for plants, animals, and humans. But when it comes to acid rain, the case is far less straightforward. When the U.S. Environmental Protection Agency established its Acid Rain Program as part of the 1990 Clean Air Act amendments, its aim was to regulate emissions of sulfur dioxide and nitrogen dioxide (the gases believed to be primarily responsible for acid rain). The data collected so far indicate that the agency has achieved its goal. Concentrations of these gases are down significantly. But as the following article suggests, reducing emissions can have some unanticipated—and unwelcome—consequences. The authors, Lars O. Hedin (now of the Department of Ecology and Evolutionary Biology at Princeton University) and Gene E. Likens (director of the Institute of Ecosystem Studies), say emissions of acidic pollutants must be cut even more drastically to counteract the damage caused by acid rain buildup. In 2005, the EPA

*announced a permanent cap on sulfur dioxide
and nitrogen dioxide emissions in several eastern
states. What effect, if any, the additional reduction
will have on forests, lakes, and streams remains
to be seen. —SW*

"Atmospheric Dust and Acid Rain"
by Lars O. Hedin and Gene E. Likens
Scientific American, December 1996

For the past several decades, scientists have been
studying acid rain and how it affects the environment.
As the harmful consequences of acidic air pollutants
became increasingly clear, governments in North
America and Europe began to regulate emissions of
these compounds. Countries in the European Union
enacted a variety of laws to control the release of sulfur
dioxide and nitrogen oxides; the Clean Air Act imposed
similar regulations in the U.S. Policymakers expected
these reductions to rejuvenate forests, lakes and streams
in many regions. In some respects, the issue seemed
wrapped up.

But the problem of acid rain has not gone away.
Why is the rain falling on parts of Europe and North
America still acidic, despite tighter controls on pollution?
And why do some natural ecosystems—in particular,
forests—show levels of damage from acid rain greater
than scientists originally predicted?

Recent findings suggest that acid rain is a much
more complex phenomenon than previously thought.

Results from several studies point to the unexpected but critical role of chemicals in the atmosphere known as bases, which can counteract the effects of acid rain by neutralizing acidic pollutants. We have found that all the attention given to acidic compounds in the atmosphere has obscured the fact that emissions of bases have also decreased. A number of factors seem to be diminishing the level of these atmospheric bases and in the process aggravating the ecological effects of acid rain. Ironically, among these factors are some of the very steps that governments have taken to improve air quality.

Acids and bases are measured by what is known as the pH scale: solutions with a pH of less than 7 are acidic; those with a pH greater than 7 are basic; those with a pH of 7 are neutral. Common acids around the home include vinegar, orange juice and beer; ammonia, baking soda and antacid tablets are all bases. Most of the bases in the atmosphere can be found in airborne particles referred to as atmospheric dust. These dust particles are rich in minerals such as calcium carbonate and magnesium carbonate, which act as bases when they dissolve in water.

Atmospheric dust particles originate from a combination of sources. Fossil-fuel combustion and industrial activities, such as cement manufacturing, mining operations and metal processing, generate particles that contain bases. Construction sites, farms and traffic on unpaved roads also contribute. Sources such as forest fires and erosion caused by wind blowing over arid soils with little vegetation are considered

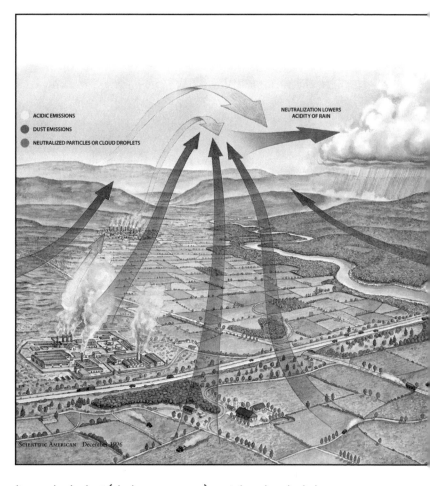

ACIDIC EMISSIONS

DUST EMISSIONS

NEUTRALIZED PARTICLES OR CLOUD DROPLETS

NEUTRALIZATION LOWERS
ACIDITY OF RAIN

SCIENTIFIC AMERICAN December 1996

Atmospheric dust (*dark gray arrows*) contains chemicals known as bases, which neutralize the acidic air pollutants (*light gray arrows*) that cause acid rain. Industrial emissions, agricultural processes, such as plowing, and traffic on unpaved roads contribute to atmospheric dust. Natural sources include forest fires and erosion by wind. Acidic pollutants derive primarily from the burning of fossil fuels in factories, cars and homes. An additional benefit of dust particles is that they deliver nutrients to forests; unfortunately, dust can cause health and environmental problems.

natural yet can still be linked to human activity.

A Natural Antacid

In the air, dust particles can neutralize acid rain in a manner similar to the way antacids counteract excess acid in an upset stomach. In a sense, when an acid and a base combine, they cancel each other out, producing a more neutral substance. Neutralization in the atmosphere takes place as dust particles dissolve into acidic cloud-water droplets or combine directly with acidic gases such as sulfur dioxide or nitrogen oxides. These reactions also generate so-called base cations—a term used to describe the positively charged atoms of elements such as calcium and magnesium that arise when mineral bases dissolve in water.

In addition to lowering the acidity of precipitation, atmospheric base cations also neutralize acid rain once they reach the ground—although the chemistry is a bit different than in the atmosphere. Small particles of clay and humus (decayed organic matter) in soil bear negative charges and thus attract positively charged cations, such as calcium and magnesium; as a result, soils contain a natural store of base cations attached to these particles. As acidic rainwater drains into the ground, the base cations give up their places to the positively charged hydrogen ions found in acids, which bind more tightly to the soil particles. Because these particles sequester hydrogen ions, the acidity of the water that flows through the soil stays low. In some soils the process becomes more complex: acid rain triggers the dissolution of toxic aluminum ions that also displace the base cations.

As long as the soil has an abundant supply of base cations, this buffering system, known as cation exchange, protects forests from the harmful effects of acid rain. But the natural reserves of base cations can become depleted if soils that are naturally poor in bases are exposed to acid rain over decades, as has been the case in regions of Europe and North America. In these areas, hydrogen ions and aluminum ions have displaced a large part of the available base cations in soils, allowing levels of aluminum to rise and leaving the soil highly acidic. Furthermore, such acidified soils can no longer protect downstream ecosystems from acid rain: waters that drain these forests carry both acids and aluminum into streams, lakes and rivers.

Dust particles may serve one other important role. Elements such as calcium and magnesium, as well as sodium and potassium—all of which can be found in mineral dust—are essential nutrients for most plants. Acid rain not only dislodges these elements from clay and humus particles, from which plants get most of their nutrients, it also washes them into rivers and streams, depleting the ecosystem of its store of minerals. With the exception of early work in the 1950s by Hans Egnér of Uppsala Agricultural University in Sweden and Eville Gorham of the Freshwater Biological Association laboratory in England, scientists have not paid much attention to the idea that the atmosphere can be a major source of base cations found in soils. Scientists have traditionally thought that the slow dissolution of minerals and rocks in deeper parts of the soil replenished base cations, in a natural process called chemical weathering.

But recent findings, including our own studies, are now revising the general view of how bases enter soils and how forests depend on atmospheric inputs of minerals and nutrients. In some forests the atmosphere actually appears to be the main source of base cations. These new results suggest that many forests are more sensitive to changes in atmospheric chemistry than scientists once believed.

Less Dust, More Damage

Efforts to reduce emissions of acidic air pollutants offered encouraging results at first: levels of atmospheric sulfur, for instance, have dropped dramatically over the past three decades in much of Europe and eastern North America. The two of us became concerned, however, that policymakers and scientists alike might be neglecting the role of atmospheric bases in their attempts to evaluate whether these reductions in sulfur compounds have benefited the environment. Considering the significance of basic chemicals to both forest growth and the prevention of acid rain, we decided to investigate whether levels of atmospheric dust have also changed over time in response to lower emissions imposed by new regulations.

Regulations to limit emissions of dust were enacted because, as scientists have known for some time, microscopic particles suspended in the air can cause a range of health problems when inhaled; they also degrade visibility and contribute to a host of other environmental problems. Governments in North America and Europe have for over 20 years designated acceptable air-quality standards for particulate matter; these regulations were quite distinct from those focusing on acidic pollution. (Atmospheric dust from

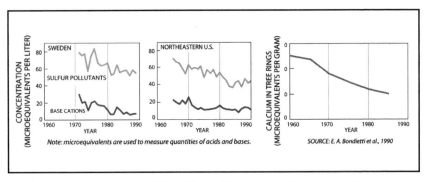

Parallel decreases in acidic sulfur pollutants and the base cations that neutralize them cancel out much of the expected benefit from reducing acidic pollutants. The authors' studies in Sweden and the U.S. provide evidence for these trends. In addition, other studies have shown that levels of the base cation calcium have decreased in the trees of a New Hampshire forest over the past several decades; such decreases in essential nutrients further weaken forests.

other sources appears to have dropped off as well: Gary J. Stensland and Donald F. Gatz of the Illinois State Water Survey have found that emissions of particles containing bases have fallen in response to less traffic on unpaved roads.)

Working together with European scientists, we began by evaluating the longest records of precipitation chemistry that can be found in eastern North America and western Europe. By measuring base cations dissolved in snow and rainwater, we can keep track of the levels of mineral bases in the atmosphere and monitor the input of these base cations into forest ecosystems. Our findings were startling: we discovered that atmospheric bases have declined at unexpectedly steep rates during the past 10 to 30 years. The longest existing North American record, collected at the Hubbard Brook Experimental Forest in New Hampshire, showed a 49 percent drop in atmospheric base cations since 1965.

On the other side of the Atlantic we found that the longest-running high-quality European record, from the forested area of Sjöängen in southern Sweden, showed a 74 percent decrease in base cations since 1971. Our analyses of several other records confirmed with few exceptions that atmospheric bases have declined precipitously across extended areas of Europe and North America.

But have these cuts in atmospheric bases been strong enough to counteract—or even nullify—the expected environmental benefits of reductions in acidic emissions? Our research indicates that this indeed has been the case. We found that the decline in bases has often mirrored the downturn in atmospheric sulfur, at rates sharp enough to offset a large part of the drop in sulfur compounds. For example, we found that the decrease in base cations canceled out between 54 and 68 percent of the reductions in atmospheric sulfur in Sweden and up to 100 percent at some locations in eastern North America [*see illustration on page 18*]. These trends mean that declines in bases have kept the atmosphere sensitive to acidic compounds despite reduced emissions of these chemicals. When we began this work, we certainly did not anticipate that reductions in one form of pollutants—dust particles— would be found to decrease the success of reductions of another pollutant, sulfur dioxide.

The numerous sources of dust particles and the often sketchy information on emissions of particulates make it difficult to determine why these sharp reductions in atmospheric bases have occurred. We do know that new and cleaner industrial techniques, developed in accordance with regulations on the release of particulate matter, have been an important factor. For example, improved combustion efficiency and the practice of scrubbing particles from smokestacks have curtailed particulate pollution associated with the burning of fossil fuels. Evaluating the contribution of more diffuse sources of dust—traffic, agricultural methods and wind erosion, for instance—has been more difficult. But our studies suggest that the decline in dust particles mainly reflects changes in human behavior as opposed to natural variations.

A Major Source of Nutrients

Scientists have watched for years as calcium, magnesium and potassium levels have dropped in forest soils around the world. For example, Leif Hallbäcken and Carl Olof Tamm, both at Uppsala Agricultural University in Sweden, have documented losses of 56 to 74 percent of the available cations in Norway spruce forests over the past 60 years. Other reports show similarly dramatic losses of base cations in England, Germany and the U.S. Several recent studies of ailing forests show that the precipitous loss of base cations can be a key factor in the phenomenon of forest decline. Ernst-Detlef Schulze and his colleagues at the University of Bayreuth have argued that depletion of magnesium in soils has played a significant role in the dwindling of spruce forests in the Fichtelgebirge of Germany. Although their evidence is less clear, researchers at Oak Ridge National Laboratory in Tennessee, led by Samuel B. McLaughlin, have found that the slowdown in growth of red spruce trees in the southern Appalachian Mountains correlates with lower availability of calcium in soils. Interestingly, small-scale experiments involving fertilization of some forests with base cations, particularly calcium and magnesium, have ameliorated damage—in the sugar maple forests of Quebec, for instance, and in Norway spruce and silver fir forests of Germany and France.

Reports such as these made us wonder whether certain soils are suffering not only because of continued exposure to acid rain but also because they do not receive enough base cations from the atmosphere. Scientists can now pinpoint the origin of base cations and trace their movements through forest ecosystems by looking at the natural isotopes of the element strontium (determined by evaluating the number of neutrons in the nucleus of a strontium atom), which can be used as a tracer for calcium. Strontium atoms that derive from the bedrock and those that come from the atmosphere tend to exist as different mixtures of isotopes. This technique has illustrated that atmospheric dust is in fact a critical source of mineral ions in many forest ecosystems.

Moreover, in certain regions, where soils tend to be damaged by acid rain or naturally low in base cations, most of the calcium appears to come from the atmosphere rather than the bedrock. For instance, we have determined that in unpolluted forests of Chile, the dominant tree species, the southern beech, feeds on calcium that originates almost exclusively in the atmosphere.

These observations suggest that many forests depend quite heavily on the atmosphere for a supply of mineral bases; the drops in atmospheric base cations have therefore led to a slower replenishment of critical bases and nutrients in forest soils. Of course, natural levels of atmospheric dust have always varied, but usually across centuries or millennia. Studies conducted by

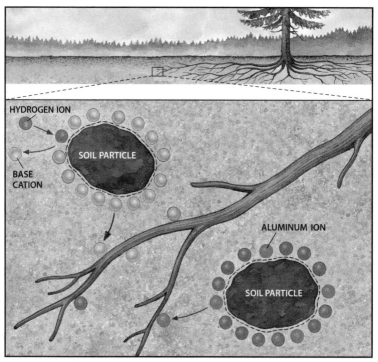

Base cations (*light gray*) in soil provide nutrients for plants, which absorb the chemicals through their roots. Typically, base cations attach themselves to particles of humus or clay (*left*). But when acid rain falls on the soil, hydrogen ions (*dark gray*) from the rain displace the base cations, which are then washed away. Over time, the hydrogen ions, together with aluminum ions (*medium gray*) released from the soil as a result of acid rain, can build up on particles (*right*). Not only do hydrogen and aluminum displace essential nutrients, but they interfere with the plant's biochemistry; aluminum in particular can be toxic.

Paul A. Mayewski and his co-workers at the University of New Hampshire on ice cores from Greenland indicate that the amounts of dust and calcium in the atmosphere have been strongly affected by climate variations over the past 20,000 years. In the coldest and driest global climates, high levels of calcium and dust prevailed, whereas wetter and warmer periods saw low concentrations. Analysis of modern trends, from around 700 A.D. to the present, suggests that current quantities of dust are relatively low compared with conditions during the past 20,000 years. One notable exception was the Dust Bowl, the extended drought of the mid-1930s in the western U.S.

Remaining Questions

As scientists have discovered the importance of bases in the atmosphere and, more recently, the link between emissions of atmospheric dust and nutrients in the soil, they have begun to paint a new picture of how forests respond to atmospheric pollution. This emerging view suggests that the effects of acid rain are more complex than expected and that the damage caused by the pollution is more serious than predicted. For instance, the widely quoted conclusion from the 1990 National Acid Precipitation Assessment Program (the most recent evaluation of the problem of acid rain by the U.S. government), that there was no clear evidence linking acid rain to forest damage, no longer seems tenable.

It is entirely feasible that continuing acid rain, in combination with limited supplies of base cations, could produce environmental conditions to which many plant species, particularly in sensitive ecosystems, have never been exposed in the course of their evolution.

Consequently, predicting how they will respond over the next several decades will be extremely difficult. And effects may not be limited to plants. Jaap Graveland and his colleagues at the University of Groningen, have noted that certain birds, such as the great tits of the Netherlands produce thinner, more fragile eggs in forests that have been heavily damaged by acid rain and have low stores of calcium in the soil.

What can we do about acid rain and atmospheric dust? Suggestions range from the improbable to the feasible. After the publication of one of our recent papers, a reader wrote proposing that forests might be saved by a hot-air balloon campaign to drop calcium-rich particles from the skies—a costly and impractical solution. Deliberate increases in the release of particulates are also unrealistic and would set back progress in air pollution control by decades. One reasonable suggestion, however, is to reduce emissions of acidic pollutants to levels that can be buffered by natural quantities of basic compounds in the atmosphere; such a goal would mean continued reductions in sulfur dioxide and nitrogen oxides, perhaps even greater than those prescribed in the 1990 Amendments to the Clean Air Act in the U.S.

The ecological dilemma of atmospheric dust will very likely be with us for some time: base cations take years to build up in soils, and it may take decades or more for forests to recover their depleted pools of nutrients, even if levels of acidic air pollution continue to fall. In the meantime, researchers and governments must develop careful strategies not only for monitoring the current health of forests but also for predicting their stability in the next century and beyond. Simple solutions do not always work in complex ecosystems.

The Authors

Lars O. Hedin and Gene E. Likens have worked together for more than a decade, examining how acid rain affects forest and aquatic ecosystems. Hedin is an assistant professor in terrestrial biogeochemistry in the section of ecology and systematics at Cornell University. In addition to his research on base cations, Hedin studies nutrient cycles in unpolluted temperate and tropical forests. Likens is director of the Institute of Ecosystem Studies in Millbrook, N.Y. He has published extensively on the topic of acid rain and on how human activities impact the environment.

Plants depend on a rich supply of nitrogen and phosphorus to survive. However, as this next article illustrates, too much of a good thing can be detrimental to coastal waters. The number of oxygen-deprived "dead zones" author Scott W. Nixon describes has doubled over the past decade. Over-enrichment has left about half of the nation's waters so choked with excessive algae that they cannot adequately support marine life. And the *risk extends beyond the water's edge. Algae release toxins that, when blown by the wind into populated areas, may put people at risk for respiratory problems and neurological (nervous system) damage. Environmental experts realize that nitrogen and phosphorus overflow from sewage treatment plants and farms must be reduced. The question is, by how much, and in what proportion? The EPA and its counterparts in Europe are continually monitoring eutrophication (the process by which a body of water becomes enriched in dissolved nutrients that stimulate the growth of aquatic plant life over animal life, usually resulting in the depletion of dissolved oxygen) and trying to protect coastal waters from its effects. Researchers are also looking into strategies to better manage animal waste and fertilizers to reduce farm runoff. —SW*

"Enriching the Sea to Death"
by Scott W. Nixon
Scientific American Presents: The Oceans, Fall 1998

The widespread pollution of Narragansett Bay began with a great celebration on Thanksgiving Day, 1871. For 10 full minutes, the church bells of Providence, R.I., rang out, and a 13-gun salute sounded. The townspeople were giving thanks for the completed construction of their first public water supply. Soon afterward clean water flowed through taps and flush toilets, liberating residents forever from backbreaking trips to the well and freezing visits to the privy. Millions learned the joys of running water between about 1850 and 1920, as towns throughout North America and Europe threw similar parties. But homeowners gave scant thought to how their gleaming new water closets would change the makeup of the oceans.

With the wonder of running water came the unpleasant problem of running waste. No longer was human excrement deposited discreetly in dry ground; the new flush toilets discharged streams of polluted water that often flowed through the streets. Town elders coped with the unhappy turn of events by building expensive networks of sewers, which invariably routed waste to the most convenient body of water nearby. In this way, towns quickly succeeded in diverting the torrent of waste from backyards and city streets to fishing spots, swimming holes and adjacent ocean shores. In many cases, the results were disastrous for the aquatic environment. And as the flow continues, society still struggles with the repercussions for the plants and animals that inhabit coastal waters.

Untamed Growth

Even a century ago the unsightly consequences of dumping raw sewage directly into lakes and bays were quite troubling. Dead fish and malodorous sludges fouled favorite beaches as sewage rode back toward land on the waves. Unwilling to return to the days of chamber pots and privies, people were soon forced to clean up their waste somewhat before discharging it.

The wastewater-treatment technologies put into place between about 1880 and 1940 removed visible debris and pathogenic organisms from sewer effluent, effectively eliminating the distasteful reminders that had once washed up on the shore. By the 1960s many treatment plants had begun to remove organic matter as well. But the various methods failed to extract the elements nitrogen and phosphorus, nutrients indispensable to human life and abundant in human waste. These invisible pollutants were flushed into rivers, lakes and oceans in prodigious quantities, and no telltale sign heralded the harm they could inflict.

As every farmer and gardener knows, nitrogen and phosphorus are the essential ingredients of plant fertilizers. Plants that live underwater often respond to these nutrients just as beets and roses do: they grow faster. Of course, aquatic plants are different from the trees and shrubs familiar to landlubbers— most are microscopic, single-celled organisms called phytoplankton that drift suspended in the currents.

Where nutrients are scarce, phytoplankton are sparse and the water is usually crystal clear. But in response to fertilization, phytoplankton multiply explosively, coloring the water shades of green, brown and red with their photosynthetic pigments. These blooms increase the supply of organic matter to aquatic ecosystems, a process known as eutrophication.

Getting the Nutrients Out

by Mia Schmiedeskamp

North Americans pour nutrients into bays and estuaries at alarming rates. Is there any way to kick this century-old habit? Recent efforts in some of the hardest-hit areas—the coastlines of Florida, North Carolina and Chesapeake Bay—show that the answer is yes.

The first line of attack is effective sewage treatment. Nitrogen can be removed from wastewater through denitrification, a process carried out by bacteria native to sewage. When wastewater managers cater to these microbes' preference for lots of food and little oxygen, the "bugs" consume troublesome nitrates and belch out harmless nitrogen gas.

Denitrification can be cost-effective as well as good for the environment. "We already see many facilities in our watershed implementing [it] even where they aren't required to," says Allison P. Wiedeman of the Environmental Protection Agency's Chesapeake Bay Program. Although capital expenditures can run from about $1 million to retrofit a modern plant to some $20 million for a complete redesign of an older one, savings in operation and maintenance offset costs over the long term.

The additional microbial treatment step cuts down on the time energy-guzzling fans must be run to aerate the sewage, for instance. Denitrification also modulates the acidity of wastewater, making some chemical additives unnecessary, and reduces the amount of sludge that must be disposed of. Currently 43 treatment plants in the Chesapeake Bay watershed have been converted to denitrification, and plans are under way to outfit 58 more in the next five years. "In the early part of the next millennium, [denitrification] is going to be standard," Wiedeman predicts.

Yet reducing nitrogen in sewage alone will not do the entire trick. In the Chesapeake Bay watershed, for instance, the goal is to reduce nutrient load by 40 percent—but only 25 percent of the nitrogen comes from sewage. Much of the rest is runoff from farmlands. Efforts to stem this flow take two forms, explains Russell L. Mader of the Chesapeake Bay Program's nutrient subcommittee: reducing the total amount of fertilizer applied to fields and keeping it where it belongs.

Land management is the key to the latter goal. "We work to minimize high-velocity flows of water that strip away soil and nutrients," Mader says. This end can be achieved by proper grading of farmland and by tillage that minimizes soil disturbance, leaving a mat of plant debris to protect the surface. And forests or artificial wetlands can serve as a buffer between field and stream, providing a place for sediments to settle from runoff and for plants to take up dissolved nutrients.

Fertilizer-reduction strategies, on the other hand, are geared at giving crops as much nutrient as they need

continued on following page

continued from previous page

but no more. Methods range from simple soil tests to computerized tractors that use satellite-based navigation equipment to direct the application of fertilizer. Mader estimates that in the Chesapeake Bay watershed alone, about 600,000 hectares (1.5 million acres) are already under various forms of nutrient management.

But some of the toughest problems are just now being recognized. Regions with high concentrations of livestock farming—where fields are fertilized by manure—are becoming overloaded with phosphorus even when their nitrogen needs are perfectly met. Reducing the phosphorus burden on the soil will leave farmers with a lot of excess manure; one of the emerging questions of nutrient management is what to do with the stuff.

Tampa, Fla., was one of the first cities to tackle the nutrient problem, with dramatic effect. In the late 1970s the city embarked on an ambitious program to restore normal life to its polluted bay, instituting a regimen of nitrogen removal from sewage and of wastewater recycling by local fertilizer manufacturers.

J. O. Roger Johansson of the city's Bay Study Group has monitored the progress since 1978. "We reduced the amount of nitrogen going into the bay by about half," he notes. "It took about two years to expend the nutrients already in the bay's sediments, and then the phytoplankton population dropped by half." Lower phytoplankton counts have been followed by fewer days without oxygen in the depths and by the return of sea grasses to the shallow waters. This bay, which was nearly ruined by human imposition, has been rescued by human intervention—good news for the Chesapeake and the many other waters still in harm's way.

Mia Schmiedeskamp is a freelance writer in Washington State.

Pollution-driven eutrophication was not recognized as a serious threat to many larger lakes in Europe and North America until the 1950s and 1960s—Lakes Erie and Washington in the U.S. are well-known examples. Why was the accelerating growth of phytoplankton a concern? After all, people welcomed the "green revolution" that fertilizers helped to bring to agriculture around that time. The difference underwater results from the precarious balance between oxygen supply and demand in aquatic ecosystems.

Terrestrial ecologists do not usually worry about oxygen, because the air is full of it: each cubic meter contains some 270 grams. And the atmosphere is constantly in motion, replenishing oxygen wherever it is used. But water circulates less readily than air and holds only five to 10 grams of oxygen per cubic meter at best—that is, when freely exchanging its dissolved gases with the atmosphere. Although fish and a number of other aquatic animals have adapted to live under these conditions, a small decrease in the oxygen content of their surroundings can often be deadly to them.

Phytoplankton floating near the surface of nutrient-rich lakes fare better in the oxygen equation. They receive ample sunlight to carry out photosynthesis during the day and have access to plenty of oxygen to support their metabolism at night. But even under the best circumstances, phytoplankton are short-lived: the tiny organisms continually die off and sink, leaving new generations growing in their place. The more abundant the bloom, the heavier the fallout to the lower depths. And therein lies the problem: the bottom-living bacteria that digest this dead plant matter consume oxygen.

When organic material is abundant in a lake and where surface and bottom waters seldom mix—for example, where winds are calm—oxygen rapidly becomes scarce below the surface. Animals that cannot escape to better-aerated zones will suffocate, and dead creatures may begin to litter the shoreline as bacteria take over the otherwise barren bottom waters. During the 1970s, such awful conditions used to regularly overcome oxygen-starved Lake Erie, which was said to be "dying."

Dead Zones

Until about 40 years ago, the oceans were thought to be immune to the combined forces of nutrient enrichment

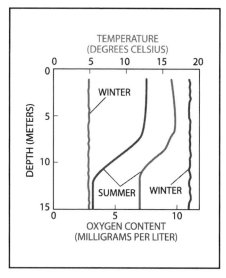

TEMPERATURE
(DEGREES CELSIUS)

DEPTH (METERS)

WINTER

SUMMER WINTER

OXYGEN CONTENT
(MILLIGRAMS PER LITER)

Sea grass is smothered by the macroalgae growing in shallow Danish waters enriched with nutrient runoff from farms and sewers. In winter, the water is well mixed, and oxygen levels are uniform throughout (*left*). In summer warm, sluggish surface water floats on top of cooler, saltier bottom water, which rapidly becomes depleted of oxygen as phytoplankton decay.

and oxygen depletion, which were then commonly observed at work in lakes. After all, the seas are vast and restless—the waste discharged from land seemed just a drop in a giant, sloshing bucket.

Scientists now know this assumption was wrong. The fertilization of coastal waters constitutes a major environmental threat to the Baltic Sea, the Gulf of Mexico, Chesapeake Bay, the Lagoon of Venice, the North Sea and a great many other estuaries, bays and lagoons in the industrial world. Most at risk are sheltered regions that do not experience winds or tides strong enough to keep the sea thoroughly mixed the whole year around. For just like nutrient-rich lakes, polluted bays and estuaries can become starved of oxygen when their bottom waters are cut off from the atmosphere.

Coastal areas are especially vulnerable to oxygen depletion because freshwater draining into the ocean from rivers and streams—often laden with nutrients—tends to float on top of denser saltwater. In summer, the surface layer becomes even more buoyant as it warms in the sun. Unless some energetic mixing ensues, the lighter, oxygen-rich veneer will remain isolated from the denser water below. In areas of weak wind and tide, such stratification can last an entire summer.

When a polluted bay or estuary remains relatively still for weeks, months or whole seasons, the difference between life at the top and life at the bottom becomes stark. The surface waters, rich in nutrients and bathed in sunlight, teem with phytoplankton and other forms of floating plant life. The bottom layers become choked with dead plant matter, which consumes more and more oxygen as it decomposes. Below the surface, entire bays can suffocate. And the problem is not necessarily limited to protected waters near the shore. Where enough nutrients arrive and currents are configured just right, even open waters can fall victim. For instance, oxygen deprivation cuts a lethal swath through some 18,000 square kilometers (7,000 square miles) of the deep waters of the Gulf of Mexico every summer, creating a barren region called the "dead zone."

The effects of eutrophication trickle up into human affairs in various ways. Bays and estuaries provide some of the richest fishing grounds, yet oxygen depletion kills fish, and nutrients may cause certain toxic varieties of phytoplankton to bloom, contaminating the shellfish that feed on them. Picturesque shores are sullied by dead fish and rotting plant waste, and the water may reek of rotten eggs as bacteria on the ocean floor spew out hydrogen sulfide.

Fertilization of coastal waters also changes life underwater in more subtle ways. For example, as the balance of nutrients changes, the mix of phytoplankton may shift in response. In particular, diatoms, which need about as much silicon as nitrogen, cannot benefit. Because pollution increases the supply of nitrogen but not the amount of silicon, these important organisms may be crowded out by other species of phytoplankton that are less useful to feeding fish and shellfish.

What is more, sunlight does not penetrate deeply into water clouded by blooms. Thick layers of phytoplankton may shade out the sea grasses and seaweeds that typically grow in coastal waters and shelter vulnerable creatures such as crabs and young fish. As a result, complex aquatic food chains may be broken apart.

Cattle, Corn and Cars

The assault on the waters of the developed world that began with urban sewage systems in the mid-1800s has only escalated since that time. Because nitrogen and phosphorus are essential for human nutrition, the rapidly growing world population consumes—and excretes—ever larger amounts of both elements. This factor alone almost doubled the release of nutrients from human waste between 1950 and 1985. And not only are there more people on the earth but also the typical diet is becoming ever richer in protein. All this protein contains abundant nitrogen, which just increases the burden on the environment when it is metabolized and finally excreted.

As the human population has skyrocketed, so has the number of animals raised for food. The count of livestock—animals that also consume and excrete large amounts of nitrogen and phosphorus—has grown by 18 percent during the past 20 years. To produce the huge quantities of crops needed to feed both humans and livestock, farmers have been applying exponentially increasing amounts of fertilizer to their fields since the 1950s. The main ingredients in these fertilizers are nitrogen and phosphorus. Rain washes these nutrients off the land and into rivers and streams, which then carry them to lakes and oceans.

Between 1960 and 1980 the application of nitrogen fertilizer increased more than fivefold, and in the decade that followed, more synthetic fertilizer was spread on land than had been applied throughout the entire previous history of agriculture. Farmers have also been raising increasing quantities of legumes (such as soybeans), which live in partnership with microorganisms that convert nitrogen to nutritive forms. Vast quantities of enriching nitrogen compounds— perhaps equal to half of what is produced as fertilizer—have become available from this source.

That there have been widespread changes in the oceans is not surprising. The dead zone that forms in

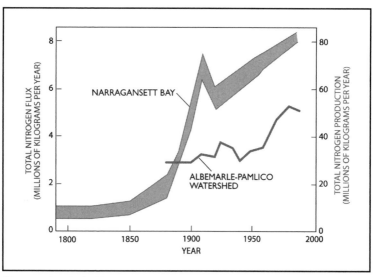

Nitrogen levels in Narragansett Bay, R.I., increased dramatically before the turn of the century, after installation of a public water supply and sewer system. Certain other watersheds did not experience a sharp rise in nitrogen levels until fertilizer use took off in the 1950s and 1960s; an example is the Albemarle-Pamlico watershed in North Carolina.

the Gulf of Mexico every summer probably results from excess fertilizer washed from farms and carried down the Mississippi. Unfortunately, such nutrient injections may be even more dangerous to coastal waters than to lakes. Research early on showed that phosphorus rather than nitrogen induces aquatic plants to bloom in most freshwater environments. This news was in a sense good for lakes, because phosphorus is more easily managed than nitrogen.

Phosphorus is chemically sticky and binds easily to other substances. Thus, it tends to adhere to soil and is less likely than nitrogen to leach out of fertilized fields. And phosphorus can be easily removed from sewage by taking advantage of the same stickiness: during treatment, chemicals are added that bind up the element and then settle out along with other sludge. Largely because of improved phosphorus removal from sewage and a widespread ban on the use of phosphate in products such as laundry detergent, the eutrophication of many lakes and rivers has been stopped or greatly reduced.

There is increasing evidence that the phytoplankton of most temperate estuaries, bays and other coastal ocean waters respond not so much to phosphorus as to nitrogen. Marine scientists still do not fully understand the reasons for this difference, but the implications are quite profound. Nitrogen washes easily from fertilized fields into streams and rivers; many sewage-treatment plants are not yet configured to remove nitrogen from wastewater; and there is an additional, copious supply of nitrogen to the oceans—the atmosphere.

Lightning has always converted a tiny amount of inert nitrogen gas, which makes up 78 percent of air, into soluble compounds that plants can take up in their roots and metabolize. But the combustion of fossil fuels has unleashed a torrent of such nitrogen compounds into the atmosphere. When oil, gas and coal burn at high temperatures in engines and electric-power generators, they produce nitrogen oxides. Rain and wind carry these soluble compounds to the earth, further enriching coastal waters already replete with sewage and agricultural runoff. In all, fossil-fuel combustion accounts for about 15 percent of the biologically available nitrogen that human activities add to the world every year.

Future Shock

In the 1990s marine eutrophication remains a problem of many wealthy nations. Countries such as the U.S. spend billions on fertilizer, automobiles, power plants and sewer systems, all of which feed nitrogen into the oceans. In fact, the amount of nitrogen available per square kilometer of land from fertilizer application, livestock and human waste alone is currently more than 100 times greater in Europe than in much of Africa.

Fortunately, at least the richer nations may be able to afford high-tech remedies. Sewage-treatment facilities that can eliminate nitrogen from wastewater are springing up, and man-made wetlands and precision application of fertilizers may stem the flow from farms [see box on page 30]. But just as people are seeing improvements in some of the worst-polluted coastal waters in the U.S. and Europe, the developing world is poised to repeat what industrial countries experienced over the past 100 years.

Part of the problem will come directly as a result of population growth. With the occupancy of the planet set to reach more than nine billion by 2050, there will be that many more mouths to feed, more fields to fertilize, more livestock to raise and more tons of waste to dispose of. Many experts predict that the release of

41

nutritive nitrogen from fertilizer and fossil fuel combustion will double in the next 25 years, most of that increase occurring in the developing world.

The United Nations Population Fund estimates that 80 percent of the rise in global population is taking place in the urban areas of Africa, Asia and Latin America. This increase amounts to about 81 million more people every year, a situation akin to spawning 10 cities the size of Moscow or Delhi. Compounding this source of urban growth is the continuing movement of people from the countryside into cities. It was city sewers that first overloaded waterways such as Narragansett Bay with nutrients, and the scenario is not likely to play out differently in the developing world. Sewers there, too, will likely carry raw sewage initially, and where treatment of these sludges does occur, it will probably not remove nitrogen for many years.

With large stretches of coastline exposed to unprecedented levels of nitrogen, it seems inevitable that ocean waters around the world will become greener, browner and redder and that there will be more frequent periods when the bottom of the sea in vulnerable locations becomes lifeless. Much of the next round of pollution will take place in the waters of the tropics, where both the corals and the fish that inhabit these delicate ecosystems are at risk. Yet it remains difficult to gauge exactly how damaging this inadvertent fertilization will ultimately prove. Scientists are still far from understanding all the ways the oceans will pay for keeping human life so widespread and abundant.

But as far as the residents of the ocean are concerned, there seems little cause for celebration.

The Author

Scott W. Nixon is professor of oceanography at the University of Rhode Island and director of the Rhode Island Sea Grant College Program. He studied botany at the University of North Carolina at Chapel Hill and received his Ph.D. there in 1970. For nearly three decades, Nixon has studied the flow of nutrients and the biological productivity of bays and estuaries, including Narragansett Bay, closest to his home.

As Pekka Haavisto knows, war not only destroys lives and homes, but also takes its toll on the environment. When this article was written, Haavisto and the United Nations (UN) Environment Program were just embarking on a long process to assess the combined environmental repercussions of the Iraq war and decades of conflict, neglect, and economic sanctions on Iraq. In a 2003 report, the UN Environment Program detailed the accumulated damage: contaminated soil and water, toxic gases from oil fires, and looted radioactive materials, to name just a few. Despite continued threats from the insurgency, the UN Environment

*Program continues to work with the fledgling
Iraqi Ministry of Environment to identify and
manage contaminated sites before they
become human health hazards. —SW*

"Cleaning Up After War"
by Marc Airhart
Scientific American, **October 2003**

During its springtime assault against Saddam Hussein,
the Pentagon played videos showing the deadly precision
of U.S. weaponry. Guided by satellites and lasers,
missiles found their targets without hitting nearby
buildings. Yet even if civilians were spared, they could
face dangers from spent munitions. For many weapons,
U.S. forces have for the past two decades relied on
depleted uranium, which, being nearly twice as dense
as lead, can penetrate materials more effectively than
conventional alloys can.

The metal, a by-product of uranium enrichment
for nuclear power plants and warheads, is toxic when
ingested and slightly radioactive, and that worries
Pekka Haavisto. "Do you think that people in the post-
conflict situation are somehow harder people and they
can take more burden?" Haavisto asks. "Or do you
think that they are human beings like us, and whatever
you can avoid, you should avoid?"

It's clear what his answer would be. The 45-year-old
Finn chairs the Geneva-based Post-Conflict Assessment
Unit (PCAU), a division within the United Nations

Environment Program. His team goes to places where conflicts have just ceased, looks for environmental trouble spots and sets priorities for cleanup and reconstruction.

The PCAU began in 1999 following the war in the Balkans (it was known then as the Balkan Task Force). Some of the NATO bombings resulted in the release of toxic chemicals. The executive director of the U.N. Environment Program, Klaus Toepfer, needed someone to determine the severity of the war pollution. He remembered that, while serving as a German environmental official, he had met a young environment minister from Finland who was enthusiastic and well respected. "So I came to the conclusion that this would be a great chance to bring Pekka Haavisto on board," Toepfer recalls.

Haavisto had recently finished his term in office and was considering returning to environmental journalism when Toepfer called. "And of course that was an opportunity to which you could not say no," Haavisto says. "And I arrived to an empty room with nobody to help me that first day."

Haavisto, who co-founded the Green Party in Finland, pulled together 60 experts from around the world. Through that summer and fall, the team searched for toxic or radioactive pollution in river sediments, groundwater, soil and air. In the end, they concluded that the war had not resulted in an environmental catastrophe. But they found four "hot spots"—industrial sites where pollution posed a threat to human health.

Since then, most of the necessary cleanup has been completed. "After Kosovo came the Serbia work and then the Bosnia work," Haavisto says. "Then we were asked to do similar work in the occupied Palestinian territories and Afghanistan and now just lately in Iraq. I don't know when I'm returning home to Helsinki."

At first, U.N. member nations were skeptical about the need for assessing a postconflict environment. "People were always saying, 'Well, why are you coming with the environmental portfolio? We have a humanitarian crisis, we have the refugees, and we have social issues and the schools,' and so on," recalls Haavisto, who talks virtually nonstop at times. But if you don't take care of the environment immediately, before reconstruction, Haavisto points out, it will be much costlier later. Plus, contaminants may prolong the suffering of people. "And I'm quite convinced that this is the approach that the international community should have in each and every region and after each and every conflict," he insists.

Larger, more chronic issues persist in places such as Afghanistan, where more than 20 years of fighting has taken its toll. Land mines continue to kill people and animals. Clean drinking water is in short supply because of drought, contamination from poorly located dump sites, past bombings and even simple neglect. Biodiversity loss and deforestation add to the environmental woes.

Haavisto's latest project is an assessment of Iraq. In a perfectly safe region, Haavisto and his PCAU team would need three months to complete the fieldwork and another two months to analyze the samples. Haavisto had hoped to be in Iraq by June, but frequent attacks on U.S. troops have delayed his efforts until August. He says that assessing Iraq will cost about $850,000, much of it from the Humanitarian Flash Appeal, a relief fund to which U.N. countries are asked to contribute.

Of major concern is the depleted uranium of some ammunition. When such a projectile makes impact, a bit of the uranium gets pulverized, turning into airborne radioactive dust that could be dangerous to breathe. Fragments of depleted-uranium weapons sitting on the ground can corrode and leach into the soil and groundwater. But the public health dangers of depleted uranium in the environment are not fully known. Some argue that it causes birth defects, cancers and Gulf War Syndrome. Military experts counter that no conclusive evidence links it to disease. But that may have more to do with the relatively recent use of the material and the lack of actual studies.

In any case, the PCAU team has begun mapping the areas exposed to the metal. Haavisto explains that the British government was providing information on where depleted-uranium ammunition had been used in southern Iraq. But the U.S. military was so far not helping in this regard. Distinguishing which depleted-uranium contamination resulted from this year's bombings and which from the 1991 Gulf War may also be hard.

Uranium is just one of several hazards in postwar Iraq. Haavisto's team will undoubtedly find that some industrial and military targets released toxic chemicals into the air, soil and water. The black smoke from burning oil trenches around Baghdad, meant to shroud targets, contained many toxic substances that might affect the soil and drinking water.

In addition, Haavisto expects to find a disaster in the Mesopotamian marshes: the nourishing water that once made this area the Fertile Crescent has been dammed up and siphoned off by the ousted regime. "It has not only influenced or affected the biodiversity but also the livelihoods and the situation of the marsh Arabs," he says.

Ironically, one of the biggest environmental problems in Iraq may stem not from direct military conflict but from a decade of U.N.-imposed sanctions. Haavisto explains that as replacement parts became harder to acquire, proper maintenance of oil drilling and production facilities became more difficult. When pipelines developed leaks, they were simply ignored, paving the way for widespread contamination of soil and groundwater.

Besides pointing out the problems, each assessment recommends specific solutions. In certain cases, it might mean just removing contaminants from soil in a certain place. In others, it might mean creating an entirely new administrative infrastructure for monitoring wildlife or habitats.

Other nations have begun seeing the value of environmental assessments. Tanzania wants an evaluation of the impact of refugees on the country. After years of civil strife, Somalia, Ivory Coast and Congo badly need this kind of appraisal. There is no shortage of work, yet "I still have a one-month contract," Haavisto remarks. "People are always asking, 'When are you finished?' And I say that I'm finishing every month on the 11th." For nearly five years, that contract has been renewed, fortunately—or perhaps, unfortunately. Remarks Klaus Toepfer: "We were still optimistic enough to believe that postconflict assessment would not be something like a growing market."

The Author

Marc Airhart is a producer for the Earth and Sky *radio series in Austin, Tex. Daniel Cho contributed to the reporting.*

2 | The Human Toll

We are accustomed to thinking of pollution as the viscous black smoke that belches from industrial plant smokestacks and spews from car exhaust pipes. But in recent years, the air outside has actually become cleaner, thanks to more stringent government regulations on industries and car manufacturers. It's the air inside we need to be more concerned about, say authors Wayne R. Ott and John W. Roberts. Building materials, household cleaning products, wood-burning fireplaces, tobacco smoke, and malfunctioning space heaters can all pollute the indoor environment. As a result, the air in our homes, offices, and schools is two to five times as polluted as the air outdoors, according to the EPA. Today, indoor pollution ranks as one of the top five risks to public health. To combat the problem, some states have passed their own versions of the Clean Indoor Air Act, banning smoking in restaurants, bars, offices, and other public establishments. But the problem of pollution in our own homes remains a trickier obstacle to overcome. —SW

"Everyday Exposure to Toxic Pollutants"
by Wayne R. Ott and John W. Roberts
Scientific American, **February 1998**

Imagine that a killer is on the loose, one who shoots his victims and flees. Police investigators would undoubtedly respond by visiting each crime scene and meticulously searching for clues. They would photograph the body, take fingerprints and question witnesses. An autopsy would recover the bullet for tests. The authorities could then use this information to establish exactly who was responsible.

But suppose the police took a different approach. What if they decided to start by examining all the guns that had recently been fired? Surely one of these weapons, they could argue, was involved. And they would be correct. They might even succeed in identifying the murderer—but not until after they had expended tremendous energy looking over a great number of firearms carried by law officers, soldiers and duck hunters. In a world of limited resources, they would probably run out of time and money before they came close to finding the culprit.

Surprisingly, officials charged with guarding the general population from toxic pollutants rely almost universally on the second strategy. Most environmental laws in the U.S. seek to control only the release of potentially dangerous wastes into the air and water, not the amount of contact people actually have with those pollutants. This focus on emissions rather than exposure essentially disregards the reality that toxic substances produce health problems only if they reach the body.

That oversight is, to some extent, understandable: for far too long, little information existed about the extent to which most citizens were exposed to the pollutants that the nation controls. Regulators seldom knew with any certainty the number of people affected by a given pollutant, the severity of exposure or the specific sources of the worrisome chemical. The result was that officials often focused on limiting pollution from the most apparent sources, such as automobiles and factories, while failing to address many other important but less obvious ones.

Fortunately, the science of assessing people's exposure to toxic substances has matured. In particular, scientists have developed highly sensitive analytical instruments and portable monitoring devices. Researchers have exploited this equipment in large-scale field studies, designed to gauge just where and how people are exposed to potentially dangerous chemicals.

Getting Personal

In 1980 one of us (Ott), along with Lance A. Wallace of the U.S. Environmental Protection Agency, launched the first serious efforts to assess everyday exposure of the general population to toxic substances. That program, carried out primarily by the Research Triangle Institute in North Carolina and other contract research organizations, later expanded to include some two dozen studies in 14 U.S. states. Using the same methods, researchers sponsored by private industry conducted similar studies in a 15th state (Alaska) and in one Canadian province. Most of these investigations employed monitoring instruments that were small and light enough for people to carry as they went about their normal activities. These devices showed which pollutants existed close by and in what concentration. In some cases, the researchers also made measurements of the food and water consumed. In certain instances, they determined the blood levels of various pollutants from breath samples.

So far these studies of "total human exposure" have examined the prevalence of volatile organic compounds, carbon monoxide, pesticides or dangerous particles in the daily lives of more than 3,000 subjects, a carefully chosen slice of the population meant to be representative of most North Americans living in urban or suburban areas. Chemical analyses of the samples were detailed enough to identify the specific chemicals to which the participants were routinely exposed. For instance, the investigations of volatile organic compounds typically tested for some 30 different chemicals, including many known to cause cancer in people or animals.

It is difficult to know whether the contacts most people have with these substances pose an especially large health risk, because the capacity for low levels of each compound to cause sickness is exceedingly hard to estimate. Still, these studies produced results that were disturbing: most citizens were very likely to have the greatest contact with potentially toxic pollutants not outside but inside the places they usually consider to be essentially unpolluted, such as homes, offices and automobiles. The exposure arising from the sources normally targeted by environmental laws—Superfund sites, factories, local industry—was negligible in comparison.

Even in the New Jersey cities of Bayonne and Elizabeth, both of which have an abundance of chemical processing plants, the levels of 11 volatile organic compounds proved much higher indoors than out. (Concentrations of the other volatile compounds tested were found to be insignificant in both settings.) The chief sources appeared to be ordinary consumer products, such as air fresheners and cleaning compounds, and various building materials.

Could everyday items with which people happily share their homes truly be more of a threat to their health than industrial pollution, even for people whose communities are surrounded by factories? In short, the answer is yes. For example, benzene—a chemical known to cause leukemia in workers continually exposed to high concentrations—is present in gasoline and in some household products. It is also one of about 4,000 chemicals found in tobacco smoke, so living with a smoker raises one's exposure to benzene enormously.

In 1985 Wallace combined all the existing information about how several hundred people located in five different states were exposed to this compound.

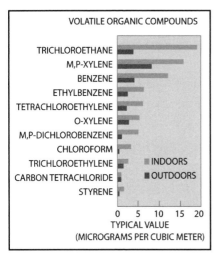

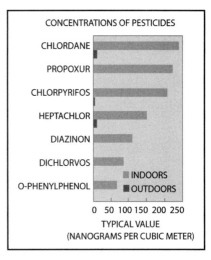

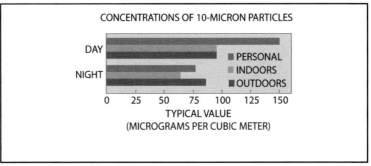

Exposure studies reveal that people come into contact with toxic volatile organic compounds and pesticides more indoors than outside. Most people's exposure to breathable particles during the day is higher than ambient levels in the air (either indoors or outside), because moving about stirs up a "personal cloud."

He found that the average concentration of benzene they inhaled was nearly three times higher than typical outdoor levels. He calculated that some 45 percent of the total exposure of the U.S. population to benzene comes from smoking (or breathing smoke exhaled by others), 36 percent from inhaling gasoline fumes or from using various common products (such as glues), and 16 percent from other home sources (such as paints and gasoline stored in basements or attached garages). He attributed only 3 percent of the average person's exposure to industrial pollution.

In contrast, government regulators usually consider only the gross amount of benzene released into the general environment, for which the largest share comes from automobiles (82 percent), followed by industry (14 percent) and domestic sources (3 percent). Cigarettes contribute only 0.1 percent of the total. Wallace's work aptly demonstrated that cutting all industrial releases of benzene would reduce health risks by only a tiny fraction. Yet even a modest reduction in cigarette smoking—the smallest source of benzene in the atmosphere—would significantly reduce the likelihood of benzene causing disease.

Many other volatile organic compounds that are quite toxic at high concentrations are also more prevalent indoors than out. For example, the chemical tetrachloroethylene (also known as perchloroethylene or "perc"), which has been shown to cause cancer in laboratory animals, is used to dry-clean clothes. Thus, the greatest exposure occurs when people live in a building with dry-cleaning facilities, wear recently dry-cleaned clothes or store such chemically laden garments in their closets. Moth-repellent cakes or crystals, toilet disinfectants, and deodorizers are the major source of exposure to paradichlorobenzene, which also causes cancer in animals. Studies have consistently indicated that almost all exposure to paradichlorobenzene comes from sources inside homes, not from industrial emissions or hazardous waste sites.

Although assessments of the risks to health are somewhat uncertain, it is clear that less contact with toxic volatile organic compounds is better than more. Most people can limit potentially harmful exposure by avoiding products that contain such pollutants. But other worrisome vapors are difficult to avoid.

For example, the major sources of exposure to chloroform—a gas that provokes concern because it can cause cancer in animals subjected to high concentrations—are showers, boiling water and clothes washers. It forms from the chlorine used to treat water supplies. Because piped water is something that people simply cannot do without, the only way to minimize household exposure to chloroform is to drink bottled water (or tap water that is run through a good-quality charcoal filter) and to improve ventilation in the bathroom and laundry.

Better airflow can also help lower exposure to carbon monoxide, a product of incomplete combustion that robs the blood of oxygen and can be particularly harmful to people with heart ailments when inhaled at levels often found indoors. Although studies conducted in the early 1980s in Denver and Washington, D.C., confirmed that carbon monoxide levels rose precipitously when people were in or near motor vehicles, other research has demonstrated that indoor appliances, such as poorly operated gas stoves, grills and furnaces, can also cause extremely unhealthful conditions—even death. Fortunately, outdoor levels of carbon monoxide have steadily declined in the U.S. in concert with the reductions in automobile emissions, as required by federal regulations. Yet further progress will be more difficult, because on the whole the U.S. population now receives greater exposure to carbon monoxide indoors than out.

Another environmental concern that appears more severe indoors is the danger from fine particles in the air. In one study, researchers used miniaturized monitors to collect minute particles in and around 178 homes in Riverside, Calif. Respondents carried devices that gathered particles 10 microns or less in diameter, ones small enough to penetrate into the lungs.

Curiously, exposures during the day were about 60 percent greater than expected from the particulate levels measured in samples of air concurrently taken indoors and outside. The higher exposures arose, at least in part, because people do not simply float through the air; rather they tend to stir up "personal clouds" of particle-laden dust from their surroundings as they move about. These investigators showed that most of these fine particles form through combustion— such as smoking, cooking, burning candles or firewood. Finding such pollutants indoors is troubling, because recent epidemiological studies have associated

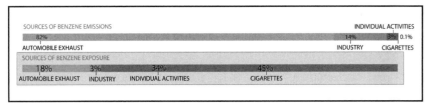

Benzene, a volatile organic compound that causes cancer in humans, is quite common. But the sources that produce the greatest quantity of emissions (automobile exhaust and industry) contribute only modestly to the exposure of the general populace, which faces a considerably greater threat from the benzene released by cigarettes, gasoline vapors and consumer products.

elevated concentrations of fine particles outdoors with premature death.

Even more disturbing were the results from two studies of indoor air contaminants conducted during the late 1980s in Jacksonville, Fla., and Springfield, Mass. In those places, investigators found that indoor air contained at least five (but typically 10 or more) times higher concentrations of pesticides than outside air—and those residues included insecticides approved only for outdoor use. Evidently, potent chemicals targeted against termites in the foundations of these houses had found their way indoors. Such poisons can be tracked in on people's shoes, or they may seep through the soil as a gas into homes. Chlordane (which was taken out of products sold for home use in 1988) and some other pesticides contaminating the air indoors caused a greater share of exposure than the amounts found on food.

In addition, people sometimes apply inappropriate pesticides directly to indoor surfaces, unaware that they are causing their own high exposures. And even the most enlightened homeowners are often ignorant of past applications of dangerous chemicals. Pesticides that break down within days outdoors may last for years in carpets, where they are protected from the degradation caused by sunlight and bacteria. This persistence is well demonstrated by measurements of the pesticide DDT (dichlorodiphenyltrichloroethane), which was outlawed in the U.S. in 1972 because of its toxicity. Despite that long-standing prohibition, Jonathan D. Buckley of the University of Southern California and David E. Camann of the Southwest Research Institute found that 90 of the 362 Midwestern homes they examined in 1992 and 1993 had DDT in the carpets.

Indeed, that study showed that the contaminants lurking in people's carpets are not restricted to pesticides. In more than half of the households Buckley and Camann surveyed, the concentrations of seven toxic organic chemicals called polycyclic aromatic hydrocarbons (compounds produced by incomplete combustion, which cause cancer in animals and are thought to induce cancer in humans) were above the levels that would trigger a formal risk assessment for residential soil at a Superfund site.

Small People, Big Problems

The pesticides and volatile organic compounds found indoors cause perhaps 3,000 cases of cancer a year in the U.S., making these substances just as threatening to nonsmokers as radon (a natural radioactive gas that enters many homes through the foundation) or secondhand tobacco smoke. And toxic house dust can be a particular menace to small children, who play on floors, crawl on carpets and regularly place their hands in their mouths. Infants are particularly susceptible: their rapidly developing organs are more prone to damage, they have a small fraction of the body weight of an adult and may ingest five times more dust—100 milligrams a day on the average.

Before 1990, when the EPA and U.S. Department of Housing and Urban Development established standard methods for sampling dust on carpets, upholstery and other surfaces, it was difficult to quantify the risk to children. Since then, however, improved techniques have allowed scientists to make more concrete statements about the degree of exposure. For example, we can now estimate that each day the average urban infant will ingest 110 nanograms of benzo(a)pyrene, the most toxic polycyclic aromatic hydrocarbon. Although it is hard to say definitively how much this intake might raise a child's chance of acquiring cancer at some point, the amount is sobering: it is equivalent to what the child would get from smoking three cigarettes.

The research also points out that, for small children, house dust is a major source of exposure to cadmium, lead and other heavy metals, as well as polychlorinated biphenyls and other persistent organic pollutants.

Carpets are most troublesome because they act as deep reservoirs for these toxic compounds (as well as for dangerous bacteria and asthma-inducing allergens, such as animal dander, dust mites and mold) even if the rugs are vacuumed regularly in the normal manner. Plush and shag carpets are more of a problem than flat ones; floors covered with wood, tile or linoleum, being the easiest to clean, are best.

One of us (Roberts), along with several colleagues, has shown that people can prevent the accumulation of dangerous amounts of dust by using a vacuum equipped to sense when no more particles can be extracted. Other of our studies have indicated that simple preventive acts can help considerably. For example, wiping one's feet on a commercial-grade doormat appears to reduce the amount of lead in a typical carpet by a factor of six. Because lead exposure is thought to affect more than 900,000 children in the U.S., the use of good doormats would translate into a significant boost to public health.

Removing one's shoes before entering is even more effective than just wiping one's feet in lowering indoor levels of the toxic pollutants that contaminate the environs of most homes (such as lead from peeling paint and pesticides from soils around the foundation). By taking such precautions to avoid tracking in dust and using an effective vacuum cleaner—one equipped with a rotating brush and, preferably, a dust sensor— people can reduce the amount of lead and many other toxic substances in their carpets to about a tenth (or, in some cases, to a hundredth) of the level that would otherwise persist.

Unfortunately, most people are unaware of the ubiquity of indoor pollution or of how to reduce it. One innovative initiative by the American Lung Association in Seattle aims to remedy that problem by training volunteers (dubbed "master home environmentalists") to visit dwellings and help residents limit domestic environmental threats.

Trouble with the Law

The many findings now available from multiple studies of people's everyday exposure all point to a single conclusion—that the same air pollutants covered by environmental laws outdoors are usually found at much higher levels in the average American residence. This situation has come about, at least in part, because the U.S. has made remarkable progress in improving the quality of outdoor air over the past three decades by controlling automobile and industrial emissions. Of the hundreds of air pollutants covered under existing U.S. laws, only ozone and sulfur dioxide remain more prevalent outdoors.

So it is peculiar that more attention has not yet shifted toward indoor pollution, the main sources of which are not difficult to identify. In fact, they are right under people's noses—moth repellents, pesticides, solvents, deodorizers, cleansers, dry-cleaned clothes, dusty carpets, paint, particleboard, adhesives, and fumes from cooking and heating, to name a few.

Sadly, most people—including officials of the U.S. government—are rather complacent about such indoor pollutants. Yet if these same substances were found in outdoor air, the legal machinery of the Clean Air Act of 1990 would apply. If truckloads of dust with the same concentration of toxic chemicals as is found in most carpets were deposited outside, these locations would be considered hazardous-waste dumps. In view of the scientific results comparing indoor and outdoor exposure, it would seem that the time is now ripe for a major rethinking of the nation's environmental laws and priorities.

The initial version of the Clean Air Act, written in 1970, focused on outdoor pollution. Even in its 1990 revision, the law has not changed much. It does not address the fact that Americans spend 95 percent of their time inside: despite all the evidence available today, the act still relies exclusively on measurements taken at outdoor monitoring stations. Many other U.S. laws pertaining to air pollution, hazardous waste, toxic substances and pesticides are similarly flawed, because they do not require accurate information on the levels of exposure people receive.

Although the absolute level of health risk posed by many toxic pollutants may be elusive, scientists can now accurately measure the exposure caused by different sources. Hence, to protect public health best, the broad suite of environmental laws should be reexamined and judged by how effectively they reduce people's total exposure rather than by how they reduce total emissions.

That effort would surely be substantial, both to recast a large body of legislation and to monitor how well the laws work to reduce exposure. But the payoff would be a dramatic reduction in health costs as well as an improvement in the economy and effectiveness of environmental regulation.

Americans concerned about toxic substances do not have to wait for their government to make these far-reaching changes. Reducing exposure normally demands only modest alterations in one's daily routine. Yet people cannot take the simple steps required without adequate knowledge. So increased education is needed. Laws requiring more detailed labeling would also help: If a product contains a dangerous pollutant, should not the manufacturer be required at least to list the chemical by name on the package? Armed with a better understanding of the toxic substances found in common products and in other sources at home, people could then make their own informed choices.

The Authors

Wayne R. Ott and John W. Roberts have long studied environmental threats to health. Ott served for 30 years in the Environmental Protection Agency, managing research on air pollution, toxic substances and human exposure. He now does research in the departments of statistics and environmental engineering at Stanford University. Roberts helped to develop the surface samplers used by the EPA to measure pollutants in carpet dust. In 1982 he founded Engineering Plus, a small firm in

Seattle specializing in assessing and controlling exposure to dangerous pollutants in the home. He works frequently with the master home environmentalist program in Seattle to help reduce the exposure of families to indoor pollutants.

Each year, more than 200,000 women are diagnosed with breast cancer and about 40,000 die from the disease, according to the American Cancer Society. Preventing breast cancer has historically been difficult because the majority of causes—namely age, heredity, and early menstruation—are impossible to control. However, within the past couple of decades, researchers have focused on a new and potentially preventable suspect: substances found in environmental chemicals that mimic the natural steroid hormone estrogen. According to the authors of this article, these environmental estrogens, or xenoestrogens, may play an important role in fostering breast cancer tumor growth. However, studies conducted on xenoestrogens both before and since this article was published have been mixed. Although some have found evidence that xenoestrogens increase breast cancer risk, others have found no link. Researchers say more studies on the subject need to be done to prove the connection exists. —SW

"Can Environmental Estrogens Cause Breast Cancer?"
by Devra Lee Davis and H. Leon Bradlow
Scientific American, October 1995

Physicians have no idea why breast cancer arises in two out of three women with the disease. The long awaited "breast cancer gene"—BRCA1—turns out to account for perhaps 5 percent of cases. Genetic inheritance and all other characteristics, or risk factors, known to increase susceptibility explain only about a third of all cases. We cannot claim to have solved the mystery fully, but a hypothesis we and our colleagues put forward in 1993 may clear up part of the uncertainty.

Our proposal, based on our own research and that of others, suggests substances we named xenoestrogens (foreign estrogens) might account for some fraction of the unexplained cases. Xenoestrogens, which are introduced into the body from the environment, mimic the action of estrogen produced in cells or alter the hormone's activity. Some xenoestrogens can reduce estrogen's effects; these varieties, which are rapidly degraded in the body, usually occur in plant foods such as soy products, cauliflower and broccoli. Other, typically synthetic, forms can amplify the effects and are long-lived. Since World War II the amplifying varieties—found in certain pesticides, drugs, fuels and plastics—have become increasingly prevalent in modern societies; they are the ones eliciting concern.

The possibility that some xenoestrogens promote breast cancer remains speculative, but evidence in its favor is accruing steadily. If the suggestion proves correct, the discovery could lead to new ways to prevent a disorder that this year will strike roughly 182,000 women in the U.S. and kill some 46,000, typically robbing 20 years of life from those who die. New preventive strategies are badly needed. No fundamental new treatments have been introduced in the past two decades, and survival rates have improved only minimally.

Xenoestrogens are not the only hormone-mimicking compounds that may contribute to breast cancer. There are indications that other endocrine-disrupting materials may also promote development of the disease. What is more, within the past 12 months, analyses issued by the German, British and Danish governments have combined with earlier studies to suggest that xenoestrogens and other endocrine-disrupting materials are also harming men and wildlife [*see box on page 70*]. Indeed, it appears that such compounds may contribute to abnormal development in animals and to a range of reproductive disorders that have reportedly become increasingly common in men worldwide—notably testicular cancer, undescended testes, urinary tract defects and lowered sperm counts.

Early Thinking

Breast cancer, like other malignancies, arises when a cell escapes the usual restraints on replication and

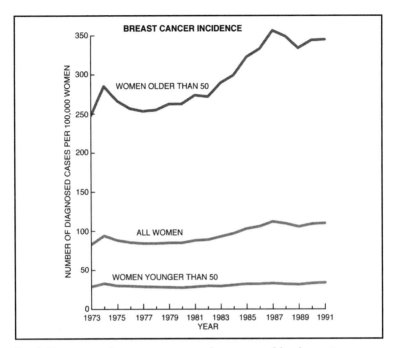

Pesticides sprayed on crops are a major source of foreign estrogens, or xenoestrogens, in the environment. The authors propose that increased exposure to xenoestrogens may explain part of the rise in the incidence of breast cancer over the past several decades in many nations. The plots above show that most of the recent rise in the U.S. has occurred in women older than 50. The data are from the National Cancer Institute's Surveillance, Epidemiology and End Results (SEER) Program, which adjusted the rates to eliminate the confounding influence of changes in the age distribution of the population over time.

multiplies out of control. This escape is now believed to require the accumulation of mutations in genes that regulate cell division and ensure the accurate replication of DNA. Hormones and other substances around the cell can also prompt abnormal cell growth.

A Message from Wildlife?

Reproductive anomalies have been found in animals born into ecosystems polluted by xenoestrogens and other compounds that disrupt the endocrine system, especially those that persist in the environment. Such anomalies include:

- Production of vitellogin, a female protein, by male fish living near outlets from municipal sewer systems.
- Death of embryos, deformities and abnormal nesting behavior in fish-eating birds living in Great Lakes regions contaminated by chlorinated organic compounds. For example, eagles and other birds have been born with crossed beaks; also female herring gulls have been found to share nests with other females and, together, to produce supranormal clutches. Nest sharing is a sign that the male population has dwindled.
- Abnormally small penises and altered hormone levels in alligators hatched in Lake Apopka, Fla., following a massive spill in 1980 of Kelthane—a pesticide that at the time (and until the late 1980s) contained DDT as an "inert" ingredient.
- Incompletely descended testes in panthers living in regions of south central Florida in which soil or water contained high concentrations of

heavy metals and persistent chlorinated organic substances.

- Deformation of shells in oysters harvested from Kepone-contaminated waters.
- Twice the rate of testicular cancer and reproductive defects in military dogs that served in Vietnam, compared with dogs that served elsewhere during the same period.

The causes of such disturbances are difficult to nail down conclusively. Nevertheless, some of the defects have been reproduced in experimental animals deliberately exposed to selected pollutants. The combined field and laboratory studies suggest that endocrine-disrupting compounds in the environment may well contribute not only to breast cancer in women but also to reproductive disturbances in men and to developmental abnormalities in animals.

We and our co-workers began to consider a role for xenoestrogens when we were puzzling over why so many women who acquire breast cancer lack most known risk factors. Among the established risks are early onset of menstruation, late entry into menopause and never having had or breast-fed a child. A well-recognized feature common to these and other factors is that they promote breast cancer by elevating total

lifetime exposure to biologically active estrogen—
principally the form known as estradiol. (Estradiol is
produced in quantity during each menstrual cycle;
some is kept in an inactive state, but the rest is able to
influence physiological functioning.) Ironically, then,
the estrogen women require for sexual development
and reproduction can harm them, by facilitating the
development of breast cancer.

Similarly, women older than 50 are more likely to
acquire breast cancer than are younger women, probably
because they have sustained longer exposure to bioactive
estradiol. Diets high in animal fat or alcohol also seem
to increase risk, probably because fat tissue can make
estrogen and because alcohol can increase production of
the hormone. Beyond estrogen exposure and inheritance
of a susceptibility gene (often signaled by having blood
relatives with premenopausal breast cancer), another
major risk factor is past irradiation of the chest with
high doses of x-rays.

If too much natural estrogen can be dangerous, we
reasoned, prolonged exposure to xenoestrogens could
probably be harmful also and might account for some
fraction of cases that had no obvious cause. The possibility that xenoestrogens could be culprits intrigued us
for another reason. We thought it could partly explain
why the reported incidence of breast cancer worldwide
(often represented by the number of cases in 100,000
women) has risen steadily since 1940. The rate is
highest in the industrial nations but is rising most
rapidly in some developing ones. Part of the rise since

the 1980s stems from better detection, at least in women younger than 65; older women have been less likely to have breast exams and mammograms, although they can benefit greatly from screening. Changes in risk factors—such as a trend toward earlier menarche (as a result of modern diets) and fewer pregnancies—influence the pattern, too. But the basis for the rest of the rise has eluded researchers.

Some investigators, such as Stephen H. Safe of Texas A&M University, doubt xenoestrogens have a role in breast cancer. They assert that people are exposed to minute quantities of individual chemicals, that the compounds are far less potent than estradiol and that plant xenoestrogens able to dampen estrogen's effects cancel out the activity of the damaging kinds. Yet these arguments are unconvincing. Although any given synthetic xenoestrogen may enter the body in small amounts, as a group the substances are ubiquitous. In the body, they also tend to persist for decades and can accumulate to high levels. In contrast, plant estrogens are degraded rapidly, and so it is unlikely that those consumed in most people's diets can negate the activity of the persistent synthetic compounds.

To understand how xenoestrogens might lead to cancer, one needs a sense of how natural, or endogenous, estradiol itself participates in the process. The steps are not entirely clear, but estradiol's ability to induce epithelial cells in mammary tissue to multiply is undoubtedly involved. These cells line the milk glands and the ducts through which milk is carried to nursing

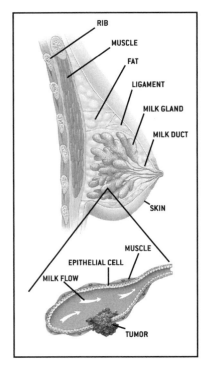

Breasts contain various tissues. Tumors are most likely to arise in the epithelial cells (*cutaway*) that line the milk glands and ducts.

infants. The hormone influences cell growth by binding to an intracellular protein known as the estrogen receptor. Complexes of hormone and receptor can bind to DNA in the nucleus and activate genes that direct cell division. Such activation speeds the rate of DNA replication and so increases the likelihood that a mutation, possibly carcinogenic, will arise and go unrepaired.

As noted earlier, estradiol is one of several forms of estrogen manufactured by the body. Conversion, or metabolism, of estradiol to other varieties of estrogen may further influence the development of cancer. At some point after estradiol is formed, enzymes alter the placement of an OH group—the hydroxyl radical—in a large fraction of such molecules. At times, the enzymes yield a product, or metabolite, that is known as 16-alpha-hydroxyestrone; at other times, they may produce 2-hydroxyestrone [*see diagram on page 83*]. The two products, whose activities differ markedly, cannot be produced at the same time; hence, whenever cells make one metabolite, the ratio of the 16-alpha type to 2-hydroxyestrone changes.

We suspect that processes favoring metabolism of estradiol to the 16-alpha form help to give rise to breast cancer, although this view is not accepted universally. For one thing, 2-hydroxyestrone activates the estrogen receptor only weakly; in analogy with "good" cholesterol, it might be called the "good" estrogen. Yet the 16-alpha variety—the putative "bad" estrogen—strongly increases the interaction of the receptor with growth-promoting genes, enhances breast-cell proliferation and perhaps damages DNA. Moreover, studies in animals and recent human trials have linked elevated levels of 16-alpha-hydroxyestrone to breast cancer.

In one of the animal projects, mouse strains that naturally acquire spontaneous breast tumors were found to have four times more of the bad metabolite in their breast tissue than did strains normally resistant to breast cancer. More recently, Michael P. Osborne, Nitin T. Telang and others at the Strang-Cornell Cancer Research Laboratory in New York City showed in a small study that breast tissue from women with breast cancer contained nearly five times as much of the 16-alpha compound as did comparable tissue from women without cancer. In the past few months Joachim G. Liehr of the University of Texas at Galveston and Ercole L. Cavalieri of the Eppley Institute for Research in Cancer in Omaha have also reported that

4-hydroxyestrone appears to be elevated in some cases of breast cancer.

The extent to which estrogens encourage the development of breast cancer may depend not only on the amount of exposure but also on the timing. Various investigations suggest that unusually high exposure to estrogen during prenatal development, adolescence or the decade or so before menopause primes breast cells to become malignant. At those times, the estrogen presumably programs the cells to respond strongly to stimulation later in life. Timing of a different sort may also explain why women who have children young seem to gain some protection from breast cancer. It is now thought that full-term pregnancy at a young age causes breast tissue to develop in ways that help epithelial cells to resist estrogen's growth-promoting signals.

How Xenoestrogens Work

Certain xenoestrogens may promote cancer by enhancing the production of "bad" estrogens. Other xenoestrogens may act by binding to the estrogen receptor and inducing it to issue unneeded proliferative signals. Chemicals with these properties may encourage the development of cancer in added ways as well. For example, there are indications that some xenoestrogens help cells to generate the new blood vessels needed for tumor growth and spread; others seem to damage DNA. Exposure at critical times may also heighten the carcinogenic effects of xenoestrogens.

How might xenoestrogens get into the body to act on breast cells? One of the most common pathways is probably through animal fat, because synthetic xenoestrogens tend to accumulate in fatty tissue. Foods from animals at the top of the food chain are likely to deliver larger doses than are foods from organisms at lower levels; hence, meat derived from animals that eat smaller animals or contaminated grass, grain or water would probably yield more exposure than would a plate of vegetables carrying residues of estrogenic pesticides. Corn oil and related polyunsaturated fats appear to have estrogenic effects and can also be a source of exposure. People who live in areas where the air or water is highly polluted by industry or by the dumping or burning of wastes might take in estrogenic chemicals simply by breathing the air or drinking contaminated water. Occupational exposures can occur also.

The first hints that synthetic chemicals could exert harmful estrogenic effects on living organisms emerged more than 50 years ago, when a number of researchers reported that chemicals in the environment seemed to affect reproduction profoundly in many species, including mink and sheep. Experimental work subsequently confirmed that DDT (dichloro-diphenyltrichloroethane) and certain other chlorinated organic pesticides—among them methoxychlor and Kepone (also known as chlordecone)—could indeed disrupt the endocrine system.

DDT was once used liberally (in fact it was some-times sprayed directly on people), but it was banned in the U.S. in 1972. Since then, levels in the environment have declined. Nevertheless, because the chemical persists in the environment for more than 50 years, it remains ubiquitous. It is also widely used in many developing nations, especially in places where malaria is prevalent, and residues may be present in some imported foods. Methoxychlor is an insecticide used on trees and vegetables, and Kepone was a constituent of ant and roach traps until it was discontinued in 1977.

During the past 15 years, experiments have shown several compounds to be estrogenic and to cause mammary tumors in animals. They include certain aromatic hydrocarbons in fuels and some PCBs (poly-chlorinated biphenyls). PCBs are long-lived chlorinated organic compounds that were once used as electrical insulators. They are no longer manufactured in the U.S. but can still be found in old transformers and have been detected in soil, water, animals and, at times, human tissue. Further, injections of DDT have been found to accelerate the growth of existing mammary tumors in male mice. Growth of such tumors in males is a sign that a chemical is unusually carcinogenic, because male rodents are generally resistant to breast cancer. Similarly, injection into male rats of atrazine, a popular weed killer often found in groundwater, increases the incidence of breast tumors.

Many experiments delivered larger doses than animals would typically encounter in nature. But data collected by Ana M. Soto and Carlos M. Sonnenschein of Tufts New England Medical Center hint that small amounts may be harmful when exposures are combined. The workers incubated breast cancer cells with a mixture of commonly used organochlorine pesticides, each at low levels. They saw greater proliferation than occurred when the compounds were added to the cells individually.

More recently, examinations of various pesticides have bolstered the proposition that certain xenoestrogens may promote breast cancer by shifting the balance of estradiol's by-products toward the bad, 16-alpha variety. In particular, we and our colleagues at Strang-Cornell found that DDT, DDE (a byproduct of DDT), atrazine and Kepone greatly increase the amount of the 16-alpha metabolite in cultured breast cancer cells. In contrast, a natural plant xenoestrogen produces the opposite effect. The compound, indole-3-carbinol (which occurs in broccoli, Brussels sprouts, cabbage and cauliflower), favors production of the 2-hydroxy metabolite. Separate work indicates that soy products behave in much the same way.

Laboratory evidence that plastics, too, can be estrogenic has emerged only in the past five years, although subtle clues vexed scientists long before that. In the late 1970s David Feldman and Aruna V. Krishnan of Stanford University found to their surprise that a form of yeast apparently produced estrogen. They then spent more than a decade trying to figure out just how this simple, single-cell organism, which had no obvious use for the hormone, managed that feat. Finally, in 1990, they found their answer: the yeast did not synthesize

Some Proved Xenoestrogens

The compounds listed below are among the better known ones that have been shown in laboratory tests to be xenoestrogens. Of these, DDT and certain PCBs have now been implicated in human studies as a cause of breast cancer. The substances that have been banned in the U.S. persist in the environment for many years and are available in some other countries. They may appear in foods imported from abroad and may occasionally travel as air pollution.

COMPOUND	USE	COMMENT
Chlorinated organic compounds		
Atrazine	Weed killer	Widely used today
Chlordane	Termite killer	Widely used before it was banned in 1988
DDT	Insecticide	Widely used before it was banned in 1972; still present in virtually everyone's body
Endosulfan	Insecticide	Widely used today
Kepone	Bait in ant and roach traps	Banned in 1977
Methoxychlor	Insecticide	A close relative of DDT
Some PCBs	Component of electrical insulation	No longer made in the U.S. but still found in old transformers
Plastics		
Bisphenol A	Breakdown product of polycarbonate	Leaches out into fluids when hot

Nonylphenol	Softener for plastics	Leaches out into fluids readily at room temperature
Pharmaceuticals		
Synthetic estrogens	Constituent of birth-control pills and estrogen replacement therapies	One drug, diethylstilbestrol (DES), was given to several million women during pregnancy before it was essentially banned for that use in 1971
Cimetidine	Ulcer treatment	————
Fuel constituents		
Aromatic hydrocarbons	Components of petroleum	Can be inhaled readily from gasoline and from car exhaust

estrogen after all. The "estrogen" was really a chemical that had leached out of the plastic flasks in which the yeast were growing. That chemical, bisphenol A, is a breakdown product of polycarbonate, which is used abundantly in many plastics. Polycarbonate may sometimes be found in the lining of food cans and in packaging for juices. Bisphenol A escapes from plastics when polycarbonate is subjected to high temperature.

The ability of bisphenol A to produce estrogenic effects in humans is evident from the fact that some men in the plastics industry have developed breasts after chronically inhaling the chemical in dust. But no one has yet learned whether it seeps into foods that are unheated or are heated to normal cooking temperatures, whether it remains active when ingested or whether it can participate in transforming normal breast cells into malignant ones.

In 1992 another plastic-related puzzle was unraveled by Soto and Sonnenschein of Tufts. In research unconnected to the effects of estrogen or xenoestrogens, they found that cultures of breast cancer cells sometimes multiplied more rapidly than was expected. Further probing revealed that a chemical used to make plastic flexible—nonylphenol—was the culprit. As was true of bisphenol A, it had escaped from the laboratory's plastic ware and, mimicking estrogen, induced growth. Related substances can be found in polystyrene containers, intravenous tubing and some detergents and household cleaners. The effects in the body have yet to be determined.

Human Findings

Like the laboratory analyses that have been performed, human studies—mainly examining organochlorine pesticides and PCBs—implicate xenoestrogens in breast cancer. Many of the earliest investigations found no association between cancer and xenoestrogens, but those projects relied on small pools of subjects and often failed to compare patients with like characteristics. Several newer discoveries imply those earlier conclusions were premature.

In one of the more recent investigations, Mary S. Wolff of Mount Sinai Medical Center in New York

Estradiol can be converted to two products that differ structurally only in the placement of one OH group (*bottom middle in diagram*). Many findings suggest that the form carrying the OH at position 16—16-alpha-hydroxyestrone—promotes breast cancer, and the form known as 2-hydroxyestrone is protective. For instance, Thomas L. Klug of Immuna Care Corporation in Bethlehem, Pa., finds that cancerous breast tissue from women harbors much more 16-alpha-hydroxyestrone than does normal breast tissue. Some xenoestrogens may contribute to breast cancer by elevating levels of 16-alpha-hydroxyestrone in breast tissue.

City and her colleagues at New York University had access to stored blood from 14,000 women. The team measured the levels of DDE in the serum of the 58 women who were eventually diagnosed with breast cancer and in the serum of 171 women well matched for age and risk factors. The samples from cancer patients had higher levels of DDE. In addition, women whose blood harbored the most DDE had four times the cancer risk of women who carried the least DDE. In another well-controlled study, a Canadian research team led by Éric Dewailly of Laval University looked at tissue from 41 women who had a breast mass removed for biopsy. Patients who turned out to have estrogen-responsive breast cancer had higher concentrations of DDE and PCBs.

Meanwhile, however, one large trial looking at DDE and PCBs has yielded what its authors have described as inconclusive results. In 1994 Nancy K. Krieger and her co-workers at the Kaiser Foundation Research Institute in Oakland, Calif., compared levels of these contaminants in stored blood from 150 women with breast cancer and 150 controls. When they combined the study's three ethnic groups—African-Americans, whites and Asian-Americans—they saw no difference between the breast cancer patients and the controls.

On its surface, this report casts doubt on our hypothesis. Yet David Savitz of the University of North Carolina argues that combining Asian women with other American women masks a troubling trend. When he reviewed the published data on each group separately, he discovered that whites and African-Americans with the highest levels of exposure to the chemicals were two to three times more likely to acquire breast cancer than were those with lower levels. Aggregating the data from the groups washed out these sharp differences because the Asian subjects with high levels of chlorinated organic compounds in their blood did not have excess cancer. This outcome in the Asians is consonant with reports that Asian women in their native lands have five times less breast cancer than do Americans, Europeans and African-Americans.

What might explain the lack of cancer in the Asian subjects? Even when living in the U.S., many Asians eat diets rich in soy products, cabbage, broccoli and other vegetables. According to at least one study, they also generally have higher levels of 2-hydroxyestrone and lower levels of 16-alpha-hydroxyestrone than do their non-Asian counterparts. It is tempting to speculate that the Asian women are protected in part by diets that favor formation of the good hydroxyestrone and minimize production of the bad, although genetic differences and other environmental factors could also be important.

What to Do?

The research that thus far ties xenoestrogens to breast cancer certainly underscores the need for further bench and clinical investigation. Some important clinical trials are already planned. Thanks largely to the organizing skills of activists, the U.S. now has a national action plan for exploring potentially avoidable causes of breast cancer, including xenoestrogens. The plan, which calls for an extensive survey of environmental influences on breast cancer on Long Island in New York State, was developed by Donna Shalala, secretary of the U.S. Department of Health and Human Services. A European project looking at the relation between diet and breast cancer is considering whether plant xenoestrogens can help prevent the disease.

But should more research be the end of it? Should government and industry wait until scientists can make a still stronger case for a link between xenoestrogens and breast cancer? We think not. Where large populations are subject to uncertain but possibly widespread risk, waiting for more and more proof of danger gambles with human health. Certainly, delays in declaring cigarettes a major health hazard contributed to millions of avoidable deaths from smoking-associated lung cancer, other lung diseases and heart disease.

Prudence dictates that several steps be implemented now. First, potential estrogenicity should be assessed for materials that play critical roles in our society, such as fuels, drugs and plastics—and for any proposed substitute agents. Second, the possible effects of estrogenic compounds on the human body should be assessed. Such tests should look at the consequences of long-term exposure and of interactions among widely used chemicals. Third, use of known inessential xenoestrogens should be curtailed.

Cancer is a complicated disease, resulting from many interacting factors that may differ from one person to the next. We realize that xenoestrogens cannot account for all breast cancer. But in contrast to many established risk factors (such as early onset of menarche and late menopause), they represent preventable causes. If reducing avoidable exposures to xenoestrogens made it possible to avert only 20 percent of breast cancers every year (four times more than are caused by inheritance of flawed genes), at least 36,000 women—and those who care about them—would be spared this difficult disease, and the public would be spared the burgeoning expenses of treatment and care. Such prospects are too tantalizing to ignore.

The Authors

Devra Lee Davis and H. Leon Bradlow have collaborated since the late 1980s. Davis has been newly appointed senior fellow and program director of World Resources Institute, a research center based in Washington, D.C. She is also visiting scientist at the Strang-Cornell Cancer Research Laboratory in New York City and was formerly senior adviser to the assistant secretary for health in the U.S. Department of Health and Human Services. She holds a 1972 Ph.D. in science studies from the University of Chicago and a 1982 master's degree in public health from Johns Hopkins University. Bradlow, who earned his Ph.D. in chemistry in 1949 from the University of Kansas, is director of the Laboratory of Biochemical Endocrinology at Strang-Cornell and professor of biochemistry in surgery at the Cornell University School of Medicine. His work has confirmed insightful research his eldest daughter undertook in her student days, before she died at age 30.

Arsenic. In crime novels and real-life murder mysteries, it has been the murder weapon of choice for many a devious criminal mind. It may surprise many people to find out just how *prevalent arsenic is in the environment. It is released naturally from Earth's crust via volcano eruptions and dissolved minerals, and discharged commercially through the burning of fossil fuels and during the manufacture of certain chemicals and metals. Consequently, arsenic is in our air, food, and water. Although the EPA and World Health Organization (WHO) have set strict standards on the amount of arsenic allowed in drinking water (no more than ten parts per billion), poor nations such as Bangladesh don't have the purification technology in place to meet such stringent requirements. As a result, arsenic has endangered between 35 and 77 million people in Bangladesh, and perhaps millions more in other countries. The WHO has referred to the Bangladesh arsenic crisis as the "largest mass poisoning of a population in history." —SW*

"Arsenic Crisis in Bangladesh"
by A. Mushtaque R. Chowdhury
Scientific American, August 2004

A cold, clear, sparkling flow gushes from the tubewell where Pinjra Begum used to collect drinking water for her family. Married at age 15 to a millworker, she had made a pretty bride. Soon, however, her skin began to turn blotchy, then ultimately gangrenous and repulsive. Her husband remarried. In 2000 she died of cancer, at 26 years of age, leaving three children.

Pinjra Begum was poisoned by the beautiful water she had faithfully pumped. In the 1970s and 1980s the Bangladesh government, along with international aid agencies spearheaded by UNICEF, undertook an ambitious project to bring clean water to the nation's villages. Too many children were dying of diarrhea from drinking surface water contaminated with bacteria. The preferred solution was a tubewell: a simple, hardy, hand-operated pump that sucks water, through a pipe, from a shallow underground aquifer. The well-to-do could afford them, and with easy loans from nongovernmental agencies, many of the poor also installed the contraptions in their courtyards. A tubewell became a prized possession: it lessened the burden on women, who no longer had to trek long distances with their pots and pails; it reduced the dependence on better-off neighbors; and most important, it provided pathogen-free water to drink. By the early 1990s 95 percent of Bangladesh's population had access to "safe" water, virtually all of it through the country's more than 10 million tubewells—a rare success story in the otherwise impoverished nation.

Alas, somebody—everybody—neglected to check the water for arsenic. As early as 1983, dermatologist Kshitish C. Saha of the School of Tropical Medicine in neighboring Kolkata (Calcutta), India, had identified the skin lesions on some patients as arising from arsenic poisoning. He traced the mineral to water from tubewells. The patients were mostly from the eastern Indian state of West Bengal, which shares some aquifers with Bangladesh; more pointedly, some were immigrants from Bangladesh. Over the next few years, environmental scientist Dipankar Chakraborti of Jadavpur University in Kolkata established that many aquifers in West Bengal were severely contaminated with arsenic. Yet the British Geological Survey (BGS) conducted an extensive test of Bangladesh's water supply in 1993 and pronounced it safe, not having tested for arsenic. That same year Abdul W. Khan of the Department of Public Health Engineering in Bangladesh discovered the mineral in tubewell water in the western district of Nawabganj.

Today around 30 percent of Bangladesh's tubewells are known to yield more than 50 micrograms of arsenic per liter of water, with 5 to 10 percent providing more than six times this amount. The Bangladesh government specifies more than 50 micrograms per liter as being dangerous. (I use this standard in the article. The World Health Organization's upper limit, which is also the recently revised standard of the U.S. Environmental Protection Agency, is 10 micrograms. Unfortunately, this amount is too small to test for accurately in the field.) That means at least 35 million people—almost one quarter of the population—are drinking potentially fatal levels of arsenic.

Another concern is that Bangladeshis may be ingesting arsenic through a second route: the grain they eat two or three times a day. In the dry months, rice fields are irrigated with pumped underground water. Recently researchers from the University of

Aberdeen in Scotland found that the arsenic content of local rice varies from 50 to 180 parts per billion, depending on the rice variety and on where it is grown. (Fifty parts per billion is the equivalent of 50 micrograms per liter in water.) A few vegetables, in particular an edible tuber containing an astonishing 100 parts per *million* of arsenic, are also contaminated. Hardly any guidelines exist as to what levels of arsenic in food might be dangerous.

And Bangladesh is not alone. The mineral occurs in the water supply of communities in diverse countries, such as India, Nepal, Vietnam, China, Argentina, Mexico, Chile, Taiwan, Mongolia and the U.S. [*see map on page 92*]. As many as 50 million people worldwide could be severely affected eventually. Arsenic in drinking water thus constitutes the largest case of mass poisoning in history, dwarfing Chernobyl.

Mineral Water

The first sign of poisoning, which may appear as long as 10 years after someone starts drinking arsenic-laden water, is black spots on the upper chest, back and arms, known as melanosis. Palms of the hands or soles of the feet become hard and lose sensation (keratosis). The patient may also suffer from conjunctivitis, bronchitis and, at very high concentrations of arsenic, diarrhea and abdominal pain. These symptoms describe the first stage of arsenicosis, as arsenic-induced ailments are known. In the second stage, white spots appear mixed up with the black (leucomelanosis), legs swell, and the

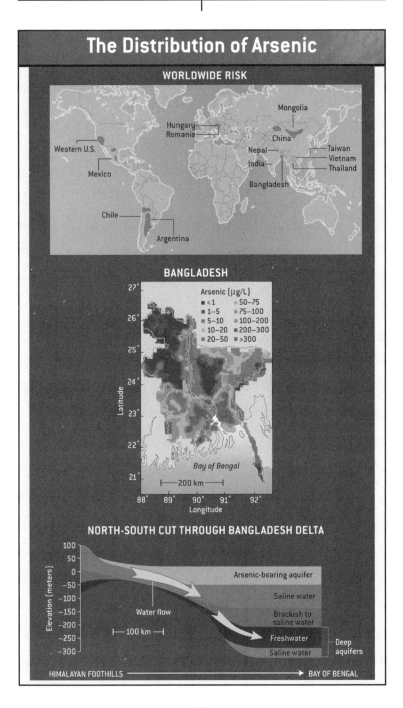

The Distribution of Arsenic

WORLDWIDE RISK

Mongolia
Hungary
Romania
China
Western U.S.
Nepal
Taiwan
India
Vietnam
Thailand
Mexico
Bangladesh
Chile
Argentina

BANGLADESH

Arsenic [μg/L]
- < 1
- 1–5
- 5–10
- 10–20
- 20–50
- 50–75
- 75–100
- 100–200
- 200–300
- >300

Latitude

Bay of Bengal

├── 200 km ──┤

Longitude

NORTH-SOUTH CUT THROUGH BANGLADESH DELTA

Elevation (meters)

Arsenic-bearing aquifer
Saline water
Water flow
Brackish to saline water
├── 100 km ──┤
Freshwater
Deep aquifers
Saline water

HIMALAYAN FOOTHILLS ──────────────────→ BAY OF BENGAL

Arsenic is found in aquifers, usually underlying river deltas, around the world (*dark gray areas on map*). In Bangladesh, arsenic levels are the highest in the south (*center*), presumably because the arsenic accumulated there when the Ganga and Brahmaputra rivers washed soil down from the Himalayas to the Bay of Bengal. The arsenic, which occurs in more recent, shallow deposits of clay, dissolves in underground water by processes that remain disputed. Aquifers deeper than 200 meters are believed to be free of the mineral (*bottom*).

palms and soles crack and bleed (hyperkeratosis). These sores, which are highly characteristic of arsenic poisoning, are painful and can become infected; they make working and walking difficult. In addition, neural problems appear in the hands and legs, and the kidneys and liver start to malfunction. In the third stage the sores turn gangrenous, kidneys or liver may give way, and in around 20 years, cancers show up.

Pinjra Begum died unusually young; she may have been drinking high levels of arsenic since childhood. One study in Taiwan found that drinking 500 micrograms of arsenic per liter of water led to skin cancer in one out of 10 individuals. The major cause of death, however, is internal cancers, especially of the bladder, kidney, liver and lung. A 1998 study in northern Chile attributed 5 to 10 percent of all deaths in those older than 30 to arsenic-induced internal cancers. These people were exposed, at least initially, to around 500 micrograms per liter. The U.S. National Research Council concluded in 1999 that the combined cancer risk from ingesting more than 50 micrograms of arsenic per liter of water could easily lead to one in 100 people dying of cancer.

Drinking water with high levels of arsenic can also lead to neurological and cardiovascular complications. The extent of poisoning depends on the dose and duration of exposure, interactions of the arsenic with other dietary elements, and the age and sex of the individual. So far no one knows the true impact of the poison in Bangladesh. Anecdotal evidence suggests tens of thousands of cases of arsenicosis and reports a "large number" of deaths. Although a few cancer cases are seen, this epidemic has yet to peak.

Unfortunately, the Bangladesh health system is unprepared for a crisis of this magnitude. Health workers can offer ointments to relieve the pain of lesions and to prevent infection, and gangrenous limbs can be amputated, but chronic arsenic poisoning has no real remedy. One suggested treatment, chelation, requires the patient to ingest a chemical that binds to arsenic and aids its excretion. Yet chelation is of limited value, because even without it the body ejects arsenic quite efficiently; besides, the patient could go right back to ingesting contaminated water. Drinking safe water, on the other hand, seems to dispel the early symptoms of arsenicosis. But providing such water is not as easy as it sounds.

The source of—and perhaps the solution to—Bangladesh's arsenic problem lies under the ground. The nation is largely a delta, formed by silt deposited over 250 million years by two great Himalayan rivers, the Ganga and the Brahmaputra. In some areas, the sediment layer is as much as 20 kilometers deep.

Most of the poisoned aquifers are shallow, however, from 10 to 70 meters deep, and lie to the south and southeast of the country. The BGS notes that around 18,000 years ago, when the sea level dropped by around 100 meters, the rivers cut deep channels into the existing sediment. In later years, these valleys filled up with a gray clay that seems to hold the poison. Older, brown alluvium, such as in the northwest or the hilly regions, is less contaminated.

An early hypothesis by Chakraborti holds that the arsenic is associated with iron pyrites and enters the aquifers by an oxidation process. So overuse of groundwater, mainly for irrigation, lowers the water tables, allowing air to reach the contaminated clay and release the arsenic. By this theory, human activity is aggravating the arsenic problem. Nowadays a rival hypothesis, that of reduction, has gained currency. According to the BGS, the arsenic is adsorbed onto particles of iron oxyhydroxide, which are reduced by organic extracts in the water itself, releasing arsenic. If so, the mineral has always been in the water. Controversy continues to rage, however: Chakraborti asserts that some tubewells he measured to be arsenic-free a decade ago are now poisoned, suggesting that complex geochemical processes are even now under way.

In response to the crisis, the government created the Bangladesh Arsenic Mitigation and Water Supply Project in 1998, to which effort the World Bank provided a loan of $32.5 million. Much of this money still lies unused because of fundamental uncertainties in how to proceed. The Bangladesh Rural Advancement Committee (BRAC), a nongovernmental organization of which I am a deputy executive director, has, however, been working since 1997 to find an answer to the arsenic dilemma.

Face Forward

Initially villagers in the two regions where we researched solutions to the arsenic problem—Sonargaon to the east and Jhikargacha to the west—would scarcely believe that their health problems arose from their precious tubewells. To ensure their cooperation, BRAC trained about 160 village women, even some who were illiterate, to test tubewell water using field kits. The volunteers tested more than 50,000 tubewells, painting red those that gave more than 50 micrograms of arsenic per liter and green those that gave less. We confirmed that they had identified 85 to 90 percent of the wells correctly. In some villages, all the tubewells turned out to be poisoned. In others, none were. Peculiarly, one tubewell might prove dangerous, whereas another close by would be fine.

The volunteers learned to identify those with skin lesions and other obvious signs of arsenicosis and to distinguish the three stages of the ailment. They found approximately 400 victims, who were subsequently examined by doctors. About three quarters of the patients were in the initial stage, but only a few had developed cancer. Most—60 percent—were male, with an average age of 36 years. Some were as young as five.

Observing the volunteers test tubewells and identify sufferers, everyone in the targeted villages became aware of this previously unknown problem.

The volunteers also worked closely with other community members and BRAC personnel to create maps that showed local sources of water—arsenic-free tubewells, ordinary wells, streams and ponds—that could possibly replace contaminated tubewells. We then tested various systems with an eye toward safety, efficacy, cost and social acceptability. Broadly, these options were water from ponds, rivers and wells treated to remove pathogens; rainwater; groundwater treated to remove arsenic; piped water; and water from very deep aquifers. Over the past few years, we have learned much about which solutions might work on a national scale. (In recognition of its contributions toward the health and development of the poor, BRAC recently received the Gates Award for Global Health, a sum of $1 million.)

Compelling reasons exist for promoting the use of surface water. It is plentiful and generally free of arsenic, down to a depth of 10 meters. Historically, the people of Bangladesh drank water from designated clean ponds. With the advent of tubewells, these ponds were neglected, filled up for building or diverted to fish culture. The pond sand filter—a sandbased system installed on the bank to remove mud and pathogens— aims to revive the use of such ponds. Unfortunately, the bacterial load is so high that although the filter reduces it by two orders of magnitude, the water still contains some contaminants. The main obstacle to this filter, however, is that most of the ponds are now employed for fish culture, and they contain toxic chemicals used for killing predatory species (before fry are released). The biocides dissipate, but the water remains unsafe for human consumption. Moreover, the community must commit to cleaning the filter every few months.

Ordinary wells also use surface water, in this case collected from within a deep hole; it normally contains few pathogens but can get contaminated with fecal matter. In contrast, rainwater is pure but not available year-round. We once thought the so-called three-pitcher method to be a brilliant idea; this simple household device filters tubewell water through two earthenware pots—containing sand, charcoal and, most important, iron chips for binding arsenic—so that safe water collects in the third pot. But the contaminated shavings need to be disposed of periodically, which is yet another problem. Larger-scale arsenic filters are expensive, and they, too, must be cleaned of poisonous sludge.

In conversations with villagers, we realized that although they want arsenic-free water, they do not want to feel that they are going back in time to methods they once discarded. Tubewells had fitted nicely with their forward-looking aspirations. In my view, any successful method must embrace this sentiment. The two options that meet this criterion are piped water and deep wells.

Over the past few years, BRAC and other organizations have implemented a pilot program to pipe water, treated at a centralized facility, to villages. People welcomed it. A recent study by BRAC, in collaboration with the World Bank, found that villagers are even willing to pay part of the cost for installation. Nevertheless, the price remains prohibitive, and implementing such a program more broadly requires organization. If Bangladesh decides to move ahead with such systems, even on a limited scale, the local government must be charged with maintaining them in conjunction with nongovernmental organizations.

The long-term solution might instead lie in deep tubewells, which extract water from aquifers 200 meters or farther underground. Much of Bangladesh consists of two overlying freshwater aquifers, a shallow one (which reaches down as far as 70 meters) separated from a deeper one by layers of clay. Geologists agree that the risk of arsenic in deep aquifers is low, but before a few million such tubewells are dug, they need to be absolutely sure. Moreover, the drilling process needs to be refined so that the deeper aquifers are not poisoned by arsenic-bearing water trickling down from the shallow aquifers through the boreholes themselves.

Such drilling technology is untested, and digging these wells will require expert guidance. Murphy's Law—if anything can go wrong, it will—seems to apply with particular vengeance in developing countries, as the arsenic problem itself indicates.

So the risk of inadvertently contaminating the deep aquifers must be carefully weighed.

Cheap Solutions for Safer Water

No perfect technology exits for providing safe water to poor communities plagued by the arsenic problem. Surface water in Bangladesh is free of arsenic but highly compromised by disease agents. The pond sand filter reduces the pathogens in pond or river water by two orders of magnitude—which is not enough. The three-pitcher method is simple and cheap: it removes arsenic from tubewell water by passing it through iron shavings. Unfortunately, disposing of the contaminated sludge is a problem for all arsenic filters, including larger, commercial varieties.

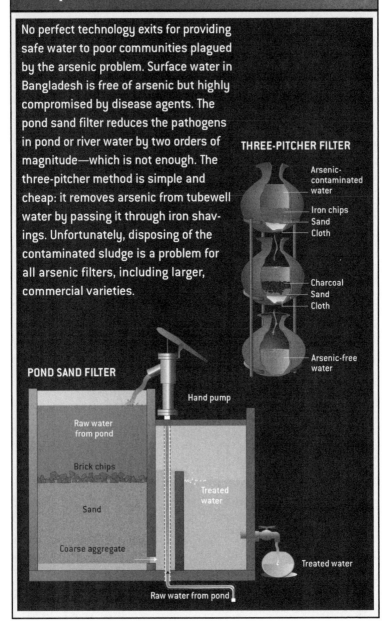

THREE-PITCHER FILTER

Arsenic-contaminated water

Iron chips
Sand
Cloth

Charcoal
Sand
Cloth

Arsenic-free water

POND SAND FILTER

Hand pump

Raw water from pond

Brick chips

Sand

Treated water

Coarse aggregate

Treated water

Raw water from pond

Money Matters

Researchers at Columbia University recently estimated that approximately $290 million will fund an integrated five-year testing, mitigation and monitoring program for arsenic all over Bangladesh. This amount, which envisages a deep tubewell in each of the country's 86,000 villages, is not too large for the benefit that will accrue, but it may be more than Bangladesh alone can afford.

Even if the money can be found, choosing and implementing a permanent solution to the arsenic problem will take several years. And Bangladesh cannot afford to wait. The country must immediately embark on a project to identify patients and provide them with safer water, in whatever way is locally feasible. In addition, we need to test every tubewell in the country. Despite everyone's best efforts, at the current rate of testing it could take several years to cover the entire nation.

In truth, even the poorest nations—perhaps especially the poorest—should check the quality of their water constantly. Ignoring this imperative is what landed Bangladesh in this predicament in the first place. Monitoring—not only for arsenic but also for manganese, fluoride, pesticides, other chemicals and pathogens—must become routine in all regions of the world where people drink water from underground.

The Author

A. Mushtaque R. Chowdhury has been involved with the Bangladesh Rural Advancement Committee, one of the

world's largest and most successful private development
organizations, since 1977. He is the founder of its research
and evaluation division and directs its arsenic mitigation
effort. Born in Bangladesh, Chowdhury received his early
education in Dhaka and his Ph.D. from the London School
of Hygiene and Tropical Medicine in 1986. He has written
extensively on health issues in the developing world.
Chowdhury serves as co-chair of the U.N. Millennium
Project's task force on child and maternal health and is
currently a visiting professor at Columbia University.

People often dive into a love affair with a new
technology or material only to regret taking the
plunge when its hidden dangers finally bubble to
the surface. Lead is one example (as in the
notorious lead paint); asbestos is another. As
James E. Alleman and Brooke T. Mossman point
out, the world's enthusiasm over asbestos came
to a screeching halt in the 1960s, after research
uncovered its threat to human health. Since
then, people who became ill from cancer and
other asbestos-related diseases have sued the
companies that manufacture and sell asbestos-
laced products to the tune of billions of dollars.
Asbestos-related litigation has driven dozens of
American companies out of business and has
prompted the government to propose an asbestos

litigation reform bill. Although its use is down considerably, asbestos continues to be a component of building materials and many other products in the United States. —SW

"Asbestos Revisited"
by James E. Alleman and Brooke T. Mossman
Scientific American, July 1997

The future for asbestos appears downright grim. After two decades of horrendous headlines, this strange fiber probably represents the most feared contaminant on the earth. It is almost certainly the most expensive pollutant in terms of regulation and removal. This year alone, remediation efforts will cost several billion dollars—a staggering outlay, even for an era of enthusiastic environmental activity. Clearly, chaos has come to the world of asbestos. The magnitude of the crisis, however, clouds a crucial irony: the problem with asbestos would never have grown so bad had we not previously thought the material was so remarkably good.

The asbestos label actually applies to a family of silicate minerals, containing silicon and oxygen, that are notable for their fibrous structure [*see box on page 106*]. Seemingly blessed with useful attributes, such as softness, flexibility and resistance to fire, asbestos was once seen as the silk of a magic mineral world. Over the centuries, people have woven asbestos cloaks, tablecloths, theater curtains and flameproof suits for protection against fiery dangers. Asbestos insulation products not only saved energy but also shielded workers from potential burns. Brake shoes and clutch facings improved safety on race cars and school buses; efficient asbestos air filters were used in hospital ventilators, cigarette tips and military gas masks. Indeed, a poignant paradox of the asbestos story stems from its previous image as a guardian of human safety.

The first references to asbestos can be traced to several ancient philosophers. One of Aristotle's students, Theophrastus, probably deserves credit for the original citation in his classic text, *On Stones*, written around 300 B.C., in which he referred to an unnamed substance resembling rotten wood that, when doused with oil, would burn without being harmed. Over the next four centuries, various Greek and Roman scholars added successive insights on this unusual rock and its ever expanding uses. In the first century the geographer Strabo identified the first Greek asbestos quarry on the island of Évvoia, where fibrous stone threads were combed and spun like wool to make an assortment of flame-resistant cloth items.

The Greek physician Dioscorides, in his first-century text *De Materia Medica*, reported that reusable handkerchiefs made of asbestos sold to theater patrons were cleansed and whitened with fire. Dioscorides' work also described an asbestos quarry on Mount Olympus in Cyprus and provided the first mention of the mineral's name: *amiantus*, meaning "undefiled," to reflect its resistance to fire. At least three other authors, including

Plutarch, indicated that the eternal flames in the Acropolis were created with asbestos lamp wicks.

The informative account given in Pliny the Elder's first-century manuscript *Natural History* includes one of the most thorough discussions of the stone written in its early history. The mineral's current name can be traced to this text: Pliny referred to *asbestinon*, meaning "unquenchable." According to Pliny, asbestos was used in a number of woven products, from easy-to-clean tablecloths and napkins to shrouds for deceased royalty placed in funeral pyres (the bodies would be incinerated by the heat even though the shrouds did not burn).

Over the next 1,000 years, asbestos continued to attract the attention of kings and chemists from western Europe to China. Even the Vatican laid claim to an asbestos burial gown reportedly found in an ancient Roman sarcophagus. Somewhere along the line, though, the fact that asbestos was a stone seems to have been forgotten.

A considerable amount of fantasy was attached to the possible source of the extraordinary fibers. Medieval alchemists started this trend with a rumor that asbestos grew as hair on fire-resistant salamanders, lending still another name, *salamandra*, to the stone. Works of alchemy frequently incorporated the imagery of an omnipotent salamander surrounded by flames. In the early 16th century France adopted this symbol as a royal emblem on flags, coins and fireplace mantles. (The French first took an interest in asbestos some 700 years earlier, when, according to popular legend,

What Is Asbestos?

Six distinct types of asbestos have been identified: actinolite, amosite, anthophyllite, crocidolite, tremolite and chrysotile. All contain long chains of silicon and oxygen that give rise to the fibrous nature of the mineral. Yet each is decidedly different in physical and chemical properties, depending on the other components of the rock, such as calcium, magnesium or iron.

The fireproof threads of asbestos are stronger than steel and quite resilient, making the stone appealing for a wide range of industrial applications. Yet the strength and resilience of asbestos also make it dangerous to human health. Asbestos fibers can penetrate bodily tissue, particularly the lungs, eventually causing tumors to develop.

The first five versions listed above (the so-called amphibolic versions) are by far the strongest and stiffest—thus making them the most dangerous. The two most common amphibolic types, amosite and crocidolite (often referred to as "brown" and "blue" asbestos, respectively), originate in remote South African mines and were once mixed with insulation and cement until regulations were enacted prohibiting the use of amphibolic asbestos. The remaining amphibolic versions—anthophyllite, tremolite and actinolite—were never commercially significant.

The sixth type of asbestos, chrysotile, once accounted for more than 95 percent of the asbestos used worldwide.

Chrysotile differs significantly in texture, composition and behavior from the other forms of the mineral. Its crystal structure is snakelike (hence its alternate name, "serpentine"), and it is noticeably softer and more flexible than the other kinds. Because chrysotile is softer and can be broken down by the body more easily than the other forms, it does not damage tissue as extensively as the five amphibolic varieties.

An estimated 20 percent of buildings in the U.S. still contain products such as shingles, cement pipes and insulation made from chrysotile asbestos. Yet well-maintained asbestos in buildings will not spontaneously shed fibers into the air. Instead decay, renovation or demolition of the structures can lead to the release of fibers. Furthermore, most studies indicate that airborne levels of asbestos in buildings—even those in which the original asbestos has been disturbed—are significantly lower than current health standards set by the U.S. government to protect asbestos workers.

—J. E. A. and B. T. M.

Emperor Charlemagne set an asbestos tablecloth on fire to intimidate his dinner guests.)

The salamander myth was just one of many. Lizard plumes and bird feathers were, for a time, each considered to be the source of asbestos. Attempts to define these fibers led to a bizarre system of nomenclature:

several dozen names were eventually assigned to the different forms of asbestos, including "mountain leather," "incombustible linen," "rock floss" and "feathered alum."

Marco Polo serendipitously brought asbestos back to the realm of science. Writing in his diary after visiting a Chinese asbestos mining operation in the late 13th century, he completely debunked the salamander theory and pegged asbestos as a stone. Georgius Agricola, one of the founders of mineralogy, provided a critical boost to the scientific understanding of the substance in the 16th century with his publication *Textbook of Mineralogy*. After carefully reviewing and updating information about the various types of asbestos, its sources and uses, Agricola offered an unusual insight: one of the very few researchers to employ an asbestos taste test, he cautioned his readers that it might "sting the tongue a little."

Asbestos Trade

In 1660, when England chartered the Royal Society, the world's scientific community was becoming increasingly fascinated by asbestos. The society published a series of eight reviews and letters on asbestos over the next 40 years. Later, in 1727, Franz E. Brückmann, a German mineralogist, wrote the first full volume on the topic; similar publications from two other leading scientists of the time, Martin F. Ledermüller and Torbern Bergman, soon followed. Ledermüller's publication was a cutting-edge treatise, depicting each of the known types of fibers with detailed colored engravings.

The range of commercial applications grew with each new publication. Fireproof coats, shirts and sleeve ruffles joined the original group of cloth items; there was also talk of making an indestructible "Book of Eternity," printed with gold on asbestos paper. Credit for another use belongs to a young inventor, Benjamin Franklin. While still a teenager, he carried a small purse woven from asbestos fiber, allegedly hoping that its contents wouldn't burn a proverbial hole in his pocket. During Franklin's first trip to England in 1724, he sold the purse to the British Museum's eventual benefactor, Sir Hans Sloane. (The purse is now in the Natural History Museum's collection.)

Even a group of devious entrepreneurs managed to earn a lucrative living during the late 1700s and early 1800s by exploiting the properties of asbestos. The most successful of these scoundrels were at the same time the most unscrupulous, selling false artifacts to a gullible audience of religious patrons. Cloth and wood relics, presented as miraculous, fire-resistant remnants of Christ's robe or cross but actually made of asbestos, were among the most popular. In a somewhat more innocent practice, a band of traveling stuntmen used fireproof asbestos gloves and capes to mystify audiences during their fiery shows. Another group, known as the Human Salamanders, was particularly famous for roasting handheld steaks while standing inside a bonfire.

In the 1820s a prominent Italian scientist converted this daredevil trick into the first truly successful asbestos business. Giovanni Aldini's ready-to-wear line

of fireproof apparel, designed specifically for urban
firemen, drew rave reviews and rapidly attracted
clients from Paris to Geneva. Shortly thereafter, asbestos
proscenium curtains began to appear, installed to
enhance stage safety and credited with saving many
lives in theater fires.

It was the steam engine, though, that made asbestos
a superstar stone. These massive machines had been
steadily pushed to their physical limits; further
improvements in safety and efficiency awaited some
breakthrough in technology. Asbestos alone tended to be
too coarse and abrasive for the engine's moving parts.
But mixed with rubber, it offered just the right combination, allowing workers to make more resilient internal
components, such as steam gaskets and packings.

By the 1860s the use of asbestos had literally hit the
roof. After dabbling in fireproof paint mixtures, a young
New York building contractor, Henry Ward Johns,
developed a flame-resistant tar paper tailor-made for
an era all too frequently plagued by building fires. This
roofing material, which blended asbestos fibers into a
tar, burlap and manila paper sandwich, paved the way
for an immense industry in asbestos-based construction
products.

Mixtures of asbestos and cement were first used in
building materials shortly after the turn of the century,
beginning with a lightweight, high-strength construction
panel invented by an Austrian engineer, Ludwig
Hatschek. Once again, because of the intense concern
about fire protection, Hatschek's invention created an

overnight sensation. Other workers soon derived several related products from Hatschek's basic formula, including synthetic slate roof shingles, corrugated wall and roof panels, and decorative wall and ceiling moldings.

Dozens of products introduced in the first half of this century incorporated asbestos. Fireproof ships were constructed out of boards of asbestos and cement. Blends of plastic and asbestos were used in buttons, telephones and electrical panels. Indeed, from its start, the plastics industry relied on the combination of plastic and asbestos; the fibers strengthened the mix, reduced weight and improved thermal resistance. Even after more advanced polymer materials began to dominate the market, asbestos remained an important binder and strengthening agent. Vinyl-asbestos tile, for instance, became a mainstay of the flooring industry. To this day, automobile brake shoes that contain asbestos are sold in repair shops around the country by mechanics unconvinced that a perfect replacement has been found.

Asbestos Man

By 1939 the public's perception of asbestos could hardly have been more positive. That year the New York World's Fair included a prominent display from the company Johns-Manville that proudly celebrated the mineral's "service to humanity." A giant Asbestos Man greeted visitors to the company's pavilion and offered a thorough indoctrination about the extraordinary traits of asbestos. The fair itself was literally draped with asbestos, from rooftop coverings to underground pipelines.

After this wave of popularity just before World War II, the demand for asbestos was on the verge of surpassing the global supply. Lacking adequate domestic reserves, the world's military superpowers found themselves heavily reliant on foreign imports. The Germans attempted to amass an adequate stockpile, covertly shipping supplies from South Africa. For a time, the Allies feared that Germany had devised a chemical substitute, although subsequent top-secret Central Intelligence Agency studies disproved these rumors.

In this country, foreign sources of asbestos—such as the exchange program set up between the U.S. and the Soviet Union by the American entrepreneur Armand Hammer and the Soviet leader Vladimir Lenin—were considered dangerously vulnerable. While Canadian mining operations tried valiantly to meet American demands, the government imposed severe nationwide restrictions on nonessential applications. Several hundred tons had to be supplied every day for uses ranging from ships' engines to auto parts for army jeeps. Parachute flares, bazooka shells and torpedoes all carried asbestos; battlefield medics even used it as an easily sterilized surgical dressing.

The global boom in construction after World War II triggered the next, and probably last, asbestos rush. Structural engineers clearly valued the strength, durability and fireproof nature of asbestos-cement products and liberally worked them into their designs. High-rise buildings became a reality in part because of an innovative spray-on asbestos coating that protected steel structures against fire-induced buckling.

The unusual properties of asbestos led to an absolutely startling range of uses. The U.S. Postal Service had it woven into fireproof mailbags. Fruit juice, wine and sugar producers purified their goods with asbestos filters. Heart surgeons used it for thread, and a toothpaste was made with its fibers. Modeling clays and artificial snow contained asbestos. Hollywood even gave the mineral a couple of bit parts, in the Wicked Witch of the West's burning broomstick in *The Wizard of Oz* and the man-made spider webs that hung across the reanimated ancient Egyptian's cave in *The Mummy*.

Escalating Health Concerns

By the time the U.S. Environmental Protection Agency opened its doors in 1970, the commercial world of asbestos had expanded into thousands of products. Annual use in this country continued to climb for another three years, hitting an all-time high in 1973 of nearly a million tons. But shortly thereafter, the history of asbestos took a negative turn, driven by escalating concerns about human health.

Problems stemming from the inhalation of exceedingly high levels of asbestos in milling and manufacturing plants had actually been observed since the turn of the century. Reports of fibrotic lung damage, known as asbestosis, in Britain's dusty textile factories led to that country's enactment of the Asbestos Industry Regulations of 1931. Over the next several decades, however, the topic drew relatively little attention from the emerging industrial health field, despite the fact that medical investigators had also uncovered a worrisome link between asbestos and lung cancer, especially in smokers.

This mood started to change during the mid-1960s as it became apparent that even low levels of asbestos posed significant health hazards; this finding implied that much larger numbers of people, including thousands of World War II–era ship insulators, might be at risk for lung damage. Disturbing results from around the world fingered the class of asbestos known as amphiboles as the principal culprits for inducing mesothelioma, a tumor found in the chest or gut. In response to these revelations, most industrial countries imposed regulations that limited exposure to just the amphiboles. But faced with increasing pressure from labor unions and ominous projections of a million-plus victims, the U.S. government chose to regulate the asbestos family as a whole.

Although the EPA's ban on all forms of asbestos was lifted in 1991, the political and legal climate for asbestos use in the U.S. is still troubled. Few people can recall this mineral's prior glory, and fewer still would ever dream of continuing its widespread use. Past generations may have considered asbestos to be an invaluable resource, but the present concern about its possible risk to human health obscures these memories.

To suggest that asbestos might still hold any redeeming qualities appears foolhardy. To qualify the mineral as a vital commodity of strategic global significance seems completely ridiculous. And yet this is precisely the case. The type of asbestos known as chrysotile (which is softer and less dangerous than the amphiboles), for example, remains an essential mineral for many crucial technologies, with the U.S. government holding military stockpiles to this day.

A prominent demonstration of this lingering importance can be found in the nation's space shuttle program. Each of the ship's solid-fuel boosters carries asbestos-impregnated rubber liners to protect the steel casings from the heat of takeoff. (The use of asbestos in aerospace applications began during the late 19th century, with the efforts to develop a fireproof hot-air balloon. A replica of an early rocket, coated in asbestos to guard against catastrophic structural failure, can be seen today on the main floor of the Smithsonian Institution's Air and Space Museum, openly defiant of the current pressures to remove all asbestos from public areas.)

Asbestos also plays a vital role in the operation of the U.S. Navy's submarine forces. These underwater vessels could not operate without some means of self-contained oxygen production; fibrous mats woven out of asbestos represent a key component in the onboard electrolytic cells that split oxygen from water molecules.

Asbestos can also be found closer to home. At least 75 percent of the chlorine used today for bleach, cleansers and disinfectants comes from chemical industries whose manufacturing processes depend on asbestos products. In fact, the very water we drink might well have been processed with asbestos-treated chlorine as well as piped through an asbestos-cement conduit on its way to our houses. Enough of the asbestos-cement pipe has been used in all 50 states since 1930 to circle the earth eight times over and still run to the moon and back.

A Rational Perspective

Admittedly, all these present-day applications (which rely mainly on the safer chrysotile form) do not require huge amounts of asbestos. Indeed, the consumption of asbestos in the U.S. has fallen by about 95 percent from the 1973 peak. Beyond our country's borders, though, many nations still consider chrysotile asbestos to be an important resource. In 1997 over two million tons of the substance will be processed throughout the world, mostly blended into asbestos-cement construction products for use in Asian, eastern European and developing countries.

The public's view of asbestos will probably never return to its previous enthusiasm. Hindsight, however, suggests that efforts to eradicate asbestos might have been somewhat misjudged and mishandled. The predicted rates of future mortality caused by both indoor and outdoor exposure to asbestos fiber now appear minuscule when compared with the risks associated with tobacco smoking and drug and alcohol abuse. The widely espoused and emotionally volatile premise that "one fiber can kill" arguably overstepped the bounds of scientific reality, triggering a purge of asbestos from schools and other buildings with dubious benefit in far too many instances.

Hoping to secure a rational perspective on the asbestos controversy, in 1988 the EPA joined Congress and a variety of concerned private institutions in asking a respected nonprofit organization, the Health Effects Institute, for an independent evaluation of the dilemma. The institute's report attempted to educate the public about the fallacies and economic consequences of rampant asbestos removal. In 1991 the American Medical Association published a second report that reached similar conclusions. These two documents emphasized that current contamination is extremely low compared with the unregulated workplace levels that originally gave rise to asbestos-related lung disease.

The global future for asbestos may hinge on supply as much as safety. Just as the ancient Greek asbestos mines eventually hit rock bottom, today's reserves are being depleted. Chemists have long searched for suitable substitutes, but a perfect solution has not yet been found. The original irony of asbestos has thus come full circle, to a present position where a substance so apparently evil could still be considered good, despite its tarnished image—quite fitting for this unquenchable stone.

The Authors

James E. Alleman and Brooke T. Mossman share an interest in the study of asbestos. Alleman, a professor at

Purdue University's School of Civil Engineering, pursues the practical applications and history of the mineral. Mossman, a professor at the College of Medicine at the University of Vermont, investigates the medical effects of asbestos.

3 Animals in the Wake

In a now famous episode of the FOX network's prime-time animated television show The Simpsons, *Bart and Lisa Simpson catch a three-eyed fish (named Blinky) in a pond near the infamous Springfield Nuclear Power Plant where their father works. The plot was likely designed to generate an uncomfortable chuckle from an audience that is all too familiar with the toll human actions can take on animal species. But in their article, authors Andrew R. Blaustein and Pieter T. J. Johnson reveal that Blinky has a real-life counterpart—the multilegged frog. Although there is no nuclear power plant to blame, the authors point out that human activity has undoubtedly played a role in the problem of frog (and other amphibian) deformities that persists in the United States and around the world. The human effect on frogs is neither direct nor easy to pinpoint. However, scientists have identified several potential culprits, from exposure to chemical contaminants and ultraviolet radiation to parasites. —SW*

"Explaining Frog Deformities"
by Andrew R. Blaustein and Pieter T. J. Johnson
Scientific American, February 2003

One hot summer day in 1995 eight middle school
children planning a simple study of wetland ecology
began collecting leopard frogs from a small pond
near Henderson, Minn. To their astonishment, one
captured frog after another had five or more hind
legs, some twisted in macabre contortions. Of the
22 animals they caught that day, half were severely
deformed. A follow-up search by pollution-control
officials added to the gruesome inventory. Occasional
frogs in the pond had no hind limbs at all or had
mere nubbins where legs should be; others had one or
two legs sprouting from the stomach. A few lacked
an eye.

The story seized national media attention and raised
many questions—among them, was this an isolated
occurrence or one facet of a widespread trend? And
what caused the deformities? As researchers elsewhere
in the country began investigating their local amphibian
populations, it became clear that this bizarre collection
of ailments was not confined to Minnesota. Since 1995,
malformations have been reported in more than 60
species, including salamanders and toads, in 46 states.
In some local populations 80 percent of the animals are
afflicted. International reports show that this phenomenon extends beyond the U.S. Surprising numbers of
deformed amphibians have been found in Asia, Europe

and Australia as well. Worldwide, extra legs and missing legs are most common.

The aberrations cannot be discounted as being a normal part of amphibian life. Research dating back to the early 1900s indicates that a few individuals in every population have defects resulting naturally from genetic mutation, injury or developmental problems. In healthy populations, however, usually no more than 5 percent of animals have missing limbs or digits; extreme deformities, such as extra hind legs, are even less common. Moreover, fresh reviews of historical records by one of us (Johnson) and new field studies indicate that deformities have become more prevalent in recent times.

Over the past eight years, dozens of investigators have blamed the increase on the amphibians' greater exposure to ultraviolet radiation, on chemical contamination of water or on a parasite epidemic. Not surprisingly, every time another report appeared, media outlets touted the new view, thus providing a misleading picture of the situation. It turns out that all these factors probably operate to varying extents, each causing particular disfigurements, and that all three may at times act in concert. Moreover, all stem in part from human activities such as habitat alteration.

Deformities undoubtedly impair amphibian survival and most likely contribute to the dramatic declines in populations that have been recognized as a global concern since 1989 [see "The Puzzle of Declining Amphibian Populations," by Andrew R. Blaustein and

David B. Wake; SCIENTIFIC AMERICAN, April 1995].
Both trends are disturbing in their own right and are
also a warning for the planet [*see box on page 126*].
Amphibians have long been regarded as important
indicators of the earth's health because their unshelled
eggs and permeable skin make them extremely sensitive
to perturbations in the environment. Chances are good
that factors affecting these animals harshly today are
also beginning to take a toll on other species.

An Early Suspect

One putative cause of the deformities, excess exposure
to ultraviolet radiation, came under suspicion almost
as soon as the malformations were discovered, because
it had already been implicated in declines of amphibian
populations and because laboratory work had shown it
to be capable of disrupting amphibian development.
This form of radiation—which can damage immune
systems and cause genetic mutations, among other
effects—has been reaching the earth in record doses
since chlorofluorocarbons and other human-made
chemicals began thinning the protective layer of ozone
in the stratosphere, a problem first measured in the
1970s. Between 1994 and 1998 one of us (Blaustein)
and his colleagues demonstrated that exposure to ultraviolet rays can kill amphibian embryos and larvae, cause
serious eye damage in adult frogs, and induce various
types of bodily deformities in frogs and salamanders.

Whether exposure to ultraviolet radiation could
disrupt leg development remained uncertain until the

late 1990s, when Gary Ankley and his co-workers at the Environmental Protection Agency in Minnesota carried out the most focused experimental research on this question to date. When the investigators shielded developing frogs from ultraviolet rays, the animals grew normal limbs, whereas tadpoles exposed to full doses of natural levels of ultraviolet radiation developed with parts of their legs missing or without digits. These deformities resembled some of those found in wild frogs from several sites around the country.

The EPA team was quick to point out, however, that ultraviolet radiation does not explain all types of leg deformities seen in nature. Most notably, it does not lead to the growth of *extra* legs, one of the deformities reported most frequently since 1995. Many laboratory and field experiments, several performed by Blaustein and his colleagues, have come to the same conclusion. Other biologists have also pointed out that many wild amphibians can avoid the continuous exposure to radiation studied in the EPA experiments. Juvenile and adult amphibians alike can move in and out of sunlight, often live in muddy water, or may be nocturnal.

Pollution's Part

As some researchers were examining the link between ultraviolet radiation and deformities, others were pursuing the influence of water pollution, such as pesticide runoff. They focused on pollution because so many of the early reports of amphibian ailments came

Overview/*Amphibian Ailments*

- Since the mid-1990s striking deformities have turned up in more than 60 species of frogs, toads and salamanders in 46 states and on four continents. The number of disfigured animals in some populations averages around 25 percent—significantly higher than in previous decades.
- Contradictory reports have blamed the deformities on increasing exposure to ultraviolet radiation, contaminated water or a parasite epidemic.
- New evidence indicates that the parasite epidemic accounts for one of the most prevalent deformities—extra hind legs—and strongly suggests that human activities such as habitat alteration are exacerbating the problem.

from areas where large amounts of insecticides and fertilizers are applied every year. By the mid-1990s numerous laboratory studies had shown that myriad contaminants can kill amphibians, but it was unclear whether they could induce extra or incomplete limb formation.

A major challenge for toxicologists is isolating a single chemical or even a group of chemicals as a likely candidate. Millions of tons of hundreds of different pollutants are applied annually in regions where deformed amphibians have been found. Yet one chemical rose immediately to the top of the list: methoprene.

First approved for commercial use in 1975, methoprene was promoted as a safer replacement for the banned pesticide DDT.

Initial concern over methoprene came from its chemical similarity to compounds called retinoids. These substances, especially retinoic acid, play an integral role in vertebrate development; too little or too much can lead to deformities in embryos. Indeed, numerous miscarriages and birth defects in humans have resulted from pregnant women's use of acne medicines that contain a retinoic acid derivative.

Some biologists suspected methoprene might have a similar effect on frogs. In a series of experiments in the late 1990s, the EPA in Minnesota did show that high amounts of retinoic acid could trigger poor formation of hind limbs in frogs, but comparable tests with methoprene caused no malformations at all. Separate field measurements also indicated that the pesticide could not be the sole cause. Methoprene breaks down quickly in the environment, and investigators found little evidence that it persists where deformities are abundant. The same is true for 61 other agricultural chemicals and their breakdown products that have been measured in locations that harbor malformed animals throughout the western U.S. Pesticides are not off the hook, however. Hundreds remain untested, and some evidence implies that certain pesticides can cause bodily damage (albeit not the formation of extra limbs).

At the moment, then, laboratory research tentatively suggests that water pollutants and ultraviolet radiation

Disfigured and Dwindling

Do the deformities explain recent declines in amphibian populations?

Frogs, toads and salamanders have been climbing up the long list of creatures in danger of disappearing from the earth entirely ever since the first reports of dwindling populations were made 20 years ago. An obvious question for biologists is to what degree physical deformities are contributing to overall population declines.

Most malformed amphibians eventually vanish from a population because they can neither escape their predators nor hunt for food efficiently. Events known to increase the number of animals that mature into disabled adults—such as the parasite epidemic that is currently afflicting dozens of sites across North America—could cause a whole population to crash, particularly if the incidence of deformities continues to increase. Although such crashes may be occurring at some sites, numerous amphibian populations have declined severely in the absence of any deformities, leaving researchers to conclude that deformities are far from the sole basis for the declines. Environmental hazards seem to be a more significant cause.

Amphibian species inhabit a wide variety of ecosystems, including deserts, forests and grasslands, from sea level to high mountains. But as diverse as their niches are, few are shielded completely from a nearly equal variety of insults that humans inflict on them. Some important amphibian habitats have been totally destroyed or are polluted to an intolerable degree. In other cases, people have introduced foreign animals that either devoured or pushed out the native amphibians.

Some of the most widespread alterations may lead to both population declines and deformities. Many studies have shown, for instance, that excess ultraviolet radiation—resulting from human-induced ozone loss in the upper atmosphere—can inhibit limb formation in amphibian juveniles or even kill embryos inside their vulnerable, unshelled eggs. In the future, global warming is expected to dry out certain suitable aquatic habitats while elsewhere encouraging the emergence of infections that produce abnormal development. When it comes to problems as pressing as these, tackling declines will most likely help alleviate the deformities as well.

—A. R. B. and P .T. J. J.

are capable of causing disfigurement. But a more potent threat appears to have a much broader impact in nature.

Prolific Parasites

The earliest hints of this threat—apparently the cause of the widespread hind-leg anomalies—turned up long before the disturbing findings in Minnesota garnered nationwide attention. In the mid-1980s, Stephen B. Ruth, then at Monterey Peninsula College, was exploring ponds in northern California when he found hundreds of Pacific tree frogs and long-toed salamanders with missing legs, extra legs and other deformities. He sounded no alarm, however, because he assumed he was seeing an isolated oddity.

In 1986 Ruth asked Stanley K. Sessions, now at Hartwick College in New York State, to inspect his bizarre amphibians. Sessions agreed and quickly realized that they were all infected with a parasitic trematode, known commonly as a flatworm or a fluke. The California trematodes—whose specific identity was unknown at the time—did not appear to kill their hosts outright, but Sessions suspected that their presence in a tadpole mechanically disturbed natural development wherever the parasites formed cysts in the body, most frequently near the hind legs. To test this hypothesis, he simulated trematode cysts by implanting small glass beads in developing limb buds of African clawed frogs and a salamander known as an axolotl. These two species, which serve as the "white rats" of amphibian biology because they are easy to breed in captivity, developed extra legs and other abnormalities—much as if they were parasitized.

As intriguing as those experimental results were, though, they could not prove that trematodes were responsible for the deformities in Ruth's specimens: African clawed frogs and axolotls are not known to have limb deformities in nature. The research that would eventually connect the dots between trematodes and extra or missing legs in frogs was conducted after the stir of 1995. At that time, Johnson pored over the scientific literature for clues to the cause and came across the discoveries made by Ruth and Sessions. Johnson and his colleagues then conducted broader surveys of California wetlands between 1996 and 1998 and discovered that ponds where tree frogs had abnormal limbs also had an abundance of the aquatic snail *Planorbella tenuis*, one in a series of hosts colonized by Sessions's trematode, now known to be *Ribeiroia ondatrae*.

Thinking that they may well have uncovered a direct correlation between a parasite epidemic and amphibian deformities in the wild, Johnson and his team immediately collected deformed frogs from the same ponds and dissected them. In every case, they found cysts of the parasite densely clustered just below the skin around the base of the hind legs. To test the idea that the trematodes were triggering the growth of the extra limbs, the researchers then exposed Pacific tree frog tadpoles to *R. ondatrae* parasites in the lab. As expected, the infected tree frogs developed deformities identical to those found in nature, including extra limbs and missing limbs. Higher levels of infection led directly to more malformations, whereas uninfected frogs developed normally.

This study turned out to be a key breakthrough in solving the mystery of deformed amphibians. Subsequent experiments, including one we conducted in 2001 on western toads, provided evidence of *Ribeiroia*'s major role in disfiguring amphibians other than Pacific tree frogs. Two studies reported last summer by Joseph M. Kiesecker of Pennsylvania State University and by a team made up of Sessions, Geffrey Stopper of Yale University and their colleagues showed that *Ribeiroia* can cause limb deformities in wood frogs and leopard frogs as well.

Other evidence indicates that *Ribeiroia* is almost always found where deformed amphibians are present, whereas chemical pollutants are found much less frequently. What is more, the parasitic infection seems to have skyrocketed in recent years, possibly reaching epidemic levels. An exhaustive literature search we conducted early in 2001 identified only seven records prior to 1990 of amphibian populations that exhibited both significant malformations and *Ribeiroia* infection.

In contrast, a field study that we published last year turned up 25 such habitats in the western U.S. alone. Among those sites, six species displayed deformities, and the proportion of affected individuals in each population ranged from 5 to 90 percent. Over the past two years, other investigators have identified *Ribeiroia* triggered deformities in Wisconsin, Illinois, Pennsylvania, New York and Minnesota, including the pond where the eight schoolchildren made headlines. Although heightened surveillance could account for some of this increase in reporting, the vast majority of deformed frogs have been found by people, often children, who were looking for frogs for reasons unrelated to monitoring abnormalities.

Not Working Alone

Scientists now understand how the life cycle of *Ribeiroia* helps to perpetuate the development of deformities in generation after generation of amphibians that are unlucky enough to share a habitat with infected snails [*see illustration on page 132*]. After the parasite leaves its snail host and enters a tadpole, it embeds itself near the tadpole's hind leg. Infected tadpoles then sprout extra legs or fail to develop both limbs. In either case, the young amphibian becomes unable to move properly and thus becomes easy prey for the parasite's final host, often a heron or egret. The parasite matures inside the bird and becomes reproductively active. Through the bird's feces, trematode eggs enter the water. When the larvae hatch, they find a snail and begin the cycle again.

If a spreading epidemic of *Ribeiroia* accounts for much, or even most, of the increase in frog deformities seen in recent years, what accounts for the epidemic? Current environmental trends suggest that human alteration of habitats is at fault. In human as well as wildlife populations, infectious diseases emerge or become more prevalent as features of the landscape change in ways that favor the proliferation of disease-causing organisms. Reforestation of the northeastern U.S., for example, has led to the emergence of Lyme disease by encouraging the proliferation of white-tailed deer, which transport ticks that harbor the Lyme bacterium. On the other side of the Atlantic,

How Parasites Can Cripple Frogs

EXCESS ULTRAVIOLET RADIATION

FERTILIZER RUNOFF

LIVESTOCK MANURE

PESTICIDE RUNOFF

EGGS

1 Parasite larvae infect snail

6 New larvae hatch, to start the cycle again

5 Adult parasites reproduce in bird

INFECTED SNAIL

ALGAL BLOOM

CYST

DEFORMED LEG

2 Larvae enter tadpole

3 Cyst forms in tadpole, disrupting development

4 Cyst waits dormant for frog to be eaten

Life cycle of the trematode *Ribeiroia ondatrae* enables the parasite to induce deformities—including extra hind legs—in generation after generation of frogs. In its first larval form the trematode infects snails (*1*). After transforming into a second free-swimming form inside a snail, the parasite embeds itself near a tadpole's future hind leg (*2*). There it forms a cyst that disrupts normal limb development and can cause the tadpole to sprout extra legs as it grows into a frog (*3*). The disabled frog then becomes easy prey for the parasite's final host, often a heron or egret (*4*). The parasite matures and reproduces inside the bird, which releases trematode eggs into the water with its feces (*5*). When larvae hatch (*6*), they begin the cycle again. Human activities can exacerbate this process, especially where livestock manure or fertilizers enter a pond and trigger algal blooms that nourish, and thus increase, snail populations. Excess ultraviolet radiation and pesticide runoff—which might cause other types of deformities when acting alone—may facilitate the cycle by weakening a tadpole's immune system and making the animal more vulnerable to parasitic infection.

—*A. R. B. and P. T. J. J.*

the damming of African rivers has led to the spread of human blood flukes that depend on snails as a host and cause human schistosomiasis. During the past several decades, alteration of habitats has also encouraged the expansion of such diseases as hantavirus, Ebola, West Nile virus, dengue fever and AIDS.

We recently showed a direct relation between human habitat alteration and sites where *Ribeiroia* parasites are especially abundant. Indeed, our survey of the western U.S., reported in 2002, revealed that 44 of the 59 wetlands in which amphibians were infected by *Ribeiroia* were reservoirs, farm ponds or other artificial bodies of water. Fertilizer runoff and cattle manure near these habitats often encourage overwhelming blooms of algae, which means more food for the snails that host *Ribeiroia* parasites. Larger populations of snails infected with *Ribeiroia* lead directly to more deformed frogs. Wading birds, the other necessary parasite hosts, are usually found in abundance at such human-made locales.

Although parasitism by trematodes is the likeliest explanation for most outbreaks of amphibian deformities, it is certainly not the only cause and may often be abetted by additional factors. At times, water pollutants or excess ultraviolet radiation may act alone to cause specific problems, such as disfigured bodies and eye or skin abnormalities. At other times, pollutants or radiation may set the stage for infection by weakening an amphibian's immune system and thus leaving the animal more vulnerable to a parasitic invasion. In yet another scenario, an increase in amphibian predators, such as fish, leeches or turtles, may create more deformities by biting off tadpole limbs.

Clearly, amphibians are subjected to a cocktail of agents that stress individual animals and then, perhaps, entire populations. The challenge to scientists becomes teasing apart these agents to understand their inter-actions. Humans and other animals may be affected by the same environmental insults harming amphibians. We should heed their warning.

The Authors

Andrew R. Blaustein and Pieter T. J. Johnson began exploring the potential causes of amphibian deformities as a team in 1998. Blaustein, who earned a Ph.D. in 1978 from the University of California, Santa Barbara, is professor in the zoology department at Oregon State University. A behavioral and population ecologist by training, he has spent the past several years investigating the dynamics of worldwide declines in amphibian popu-lations, specifically addressing the effects of ultraviolet radiation, pollutants, pathogens and nonnative species. Johnson, a doctoral candidate at the Center for Limnology at the University of Wisconsin–Madison, studies human influences on emerging diseases in aquatic environments.

On March 24, 1989, the Exxon Valdez *tanker ran aground on Bligh Reef, spilling 11 million gallons*

*(41,639,532 liters) of crude oil into Prince William
Sound, Alaska. The nation's worst ecological
disaster transformed the once pristine coastline
into an ecological nightmare. A thick, oily coat
covered 1,000 miles (1,609 km) of wilderness,
killing some 250,000 waterbirds and nearly
3,000 sea otters. The cost of the cleanup reached
into the billions of dollars, but the environmental
cost has been immeasurable. The* Exxon Valdez
*spill has come to symbolize the precarious rela-
tionship between humans and the environment.
When the accident occurred, scientists and
environmentalists wondered whether the local
ecosystem would ever recover. Now, nearly two
decades later, progress has been made, but it's
clear that the sea otters of Prince William Sound
are still paying the price for our actions. —SW*

"The Oil and the Otter"
by Sonya Senkowsky
Scientific American, May 2004

It has been 15 years since the *Exxon Valdez* oiled
Alaska's Prince William Sound, and more than 12 since
the last of the official restoration workers took off
their orange slickers and headed home. But at least one
cleanup crew never left the Sound: sea otters. The
creatures, which were hit especially hard by the first
effects of the spill, continue to feed on clams and other
food in areas that still contain pockets of oil. Their

diligent digging is helping release trapped petroleum—which appears to be sickening them. Ecologists are left with a dilemma: remove the oil (and possibly cause more harm to the Sound) or let the animals continue to do the dirty work and pay the price.

Scientists had originally predicted that any remaining oil would have been carried by waves to shorelines by now. There exposure to air would transform the oil into a hardened asphalt residue lacking the more volatile and toxic components. "The assumption was that the oil wasn't subsurface, it wasn't low, it was up there in that 'bathtub ring,' and that's where the cleaning effort was focused," explains Stanley D. Rice, a laboratory program manager with the National Oceanic and Atmospheric Administration's Alaska Fisheries Science Center in Juneau.

But in 2001, with some animals continuing to show indications of oil exposure, NOAA researchers dug into those beaches and found far more *Exxon Valdez* oil than expected—much of it still liquid—in about 70 percent of the sites. The remaining residue "still has a pretty high complement of the toxic components of oil," remarks team leader Jeffrey W. Short.

Sea otters, which feed on clams, mussels and other invertebrates, reach their prey by diving and digging underwater pits. One otter can create thousands of pits in a year, moving five to seven cubic yards of sediment a day. These excavations release oil from surrounding sediment, helping it disperse, explains U.S. Geological Survey research wildlife biologist James L. Bodkin. He has been studying a group of about 70 sea otters from northern Knight Island, a region that lost 90 percent of its sea otter population after the spill. The otters are no longer becoming coated in oil and dying from hypothermia, but there is evidence that they are ingesting the contaminants. Researchers have recorded life spans reduced by between 10 and 40 percent compared with before the spill and noted swollen and discolored livers in some dead otters.

The sacrifices of today's sea otters, however, should have their benefits, Rice observes: "The [otters] that are new and coming along, they're going to be entering a habitat that's cleaner." Decreasing levels of an enzyme called cytochrome P450-1A in the animals' blood, produced in response to toxic chemicals, indicate that an end to the prolonged oil exposure is near, according to USGS physiologist Brenda E. Ballachey and Purdue University pathologist Paul W. Snyder. "While they're still being exposed, there is less and less oil there every year," Rice notes.

With the possibility of seeking further restoration funds from Exxon on the horizon, scientists are debating whether a cleanup makes sense. "I think that if we had asked this question and had the data we have now several years ago, we probably would be out there cleaning up," Rice states. The effort generally involves mechanical tilling—essentially, plowing the affected area with heavy machinery. The method turns the ground and releases trapped oil, which is then broken down by microorganisms.

But the time may be fast approaching, Rice adds, when such intervention may not be wise. Although human cleanup efforts would more quickly make feeding safer for sea otters and other foragers, such as harlequin ducks, they would physically disrupt the environment and would not be beneficial to all organisms. "Maybe on some marginal beaches, you would do more harm than good," Rice surmises. "What might be a good idea for otters may not be a good idea for a clam or a mussel. There is no obvious choice."

The Author

Sonya Senkowsky [is] based in Anchorage, Alaska.

The majestic beluga whale once flourished in the St. Lawrence River, the body of water that connects the Great Lakes to the Atlantic Ocean. Today, only a few hundred of these whales still inhabit the St. Lawrence—the victims, scientists say, of human-spawned pollution. The Canadian government has designated the beluga whale as an endangered species, and is working to recover the beluga population to the point where it is no longer threatened by human activities. To that end, it created the Saguenay St. Lawrence Marine Park in 1998 as a sanctuary for the belugas. In recent years, the beluga *whales have experienced a slight resurgence. But scientists worry that other hazards—from coastal development to the intrusion of whale- watching boats—will continue to threaten this already imperiled species. —SW*

"The Beluga Whales of the St. Lawrence River"
by Pierre Béland
Scientific American, May 1996

In 1535, on his second voyage to America, the French explorer Jacques Cartier sailed up the St. Lawrence River, guided by two Amerindians. Beyond the mouth of the Saguenay River, adverse winds and tidal currents stalled his progress for a full day. Cartier was forced to moor for the night near a low-lying island in the middle of the river. In the morning, he was startled to see large white porpoises surrounding the ship. The native pilots said they were good to eat and called them *Adothuys*. The animals were beluga whales, an Arctic species that had lived in the St. Lawrence for millennia.

These small, toothed whales first came to the river from the Atlantic Ocean, shortly after the Ice Age ended. When the climate warmed, the Atlantic rose, flooding much of North America's eastern seaboard. The water washed over a huge area of land beyond the Gulf of St. Lawrence, almost as far as the Great Lakes and into New York and Vermont. Many species of seals and whales ventured into this inland sea, called the Champlain. In time, the land reemerged, the basin dried and the St. Lawrence took form.

Belugas and other whales continued to swim up the estuary and the river as far as they could, but they did not roam undisturbed for long. About 8,500 years ago nomadic tribes came to the edge of the river from the southwest and gathered next to shores where the belugas passed in the summer. There the people made seasonal dwellings, remnants of which are now buried under the grass and soil, along with bones from the seals and belugas they hunted.

In the 1600s Basque sailors came ashore near the Saguenay to render right whales and probably beluga whales as well. The sailors were followed in the next century by fur traders and settlers, for whom fishing provided a good income. The representative for the king of France gave concessions for catching belugas to a few hunters, who typically used fixed weir nets. These giant meshings took advantage of the falling tides to trap belugas over the river's extensive mudflats. By 1721 there were 15 such fisheries on both shores of the St. Lawrence.

For some communities, hunting belugas became a way of life, and the whale became a subject of lore. One tale has it that after catching more than 100 belugas in a single day, a village held a party in a barn near the river. Rum, whiskey and wine kept everyone lively, and laughter and music wafted over the beach, where the rising tide had started to lap at the dead whales. Around midnight, one reveler saw fleshless hands trying to seize the dancers. Everyone fled from the barn to find with dismay that the tide had reclaimed their catch. Rising from the moonlit waves, human ghosts appeared, riding the whales. The belugas' eyes shone like hot coals, and their blowholes spit flames as they swam away into the night, leaving glowing trails on the dark water.

No one knows how many belugas were killed before the 1800s. It has been estimated, though, that between 1866 and 1960 some 16,200 belugas, or an average of 172 a year, were landed. This annual yield suggests that the population must have been 5,000 to 10,000 strong near the turn of the 20th century. When catches became sparse and the demand for whale products waned, the St. Lawrence beluga was almost forgotten. By the 1970s, it is now believed, there were only 500 of the whales left.

In 1979 the Canadian government afforded the whales total protection from hunters. Despite that measure, the population has not recovered. There are still only 500 whales in the St. Lawrence today. Why this number fails to increase has been a mystery. Some marine biologists have pointed to low reproductive rates among the small population or to the degradation of their habitat by hydroelectric projects. But over the past dozen years, my colleagues and I have uncovered another reason.

Victims of Pollution

My investigations began in the fall of 1982, when I went with a local veterinarian, Daniel Martineau, to see a dead beluga beached on the St. Lawrence shore. The whale was relatively small but stood out clearly on a bed of dark pebbles in the late afternoon sun. It seemed smooth as plastic and whiter than the froth on the breaking surf. "Let's open it," Martineau suggested. The subsequent laboratory work showed that the whale had probably died from renal failure. Tissue samples revealed that it was heavily contaminated with mercury and lead as well as polychlorobiphenyls (PCBs), DDT, Mirex and other pesticides. Two dead belugas found later that same season were similarly poisoned.

In a way, the discovery was nothing new. Many scientists had documented high levels of PCBs and DDT in harbor seals and harbor porpoises elsewhere. These compounds, known as organohalogens, are highly soluble in lipids. Because they are not broken down in an animal's body, they accumulate in fatty tissues. The chemicals travel up the food chain, ultimately reaching the highest levels in top predators. A vast literature described sundry diseases associated with organohalogens—among them liver damage, gastric erosions, lesions of the skin and glands, and hormonal imbalances. But during the early 1980s, most experts believed that organohalogens posed little threat to marine mammals.

Still, curious as to why the population of St. Lawrence belugas had remained low despite protective measures, we continued our studies. Over the next 15 years or so, we recorded 179 deaths and

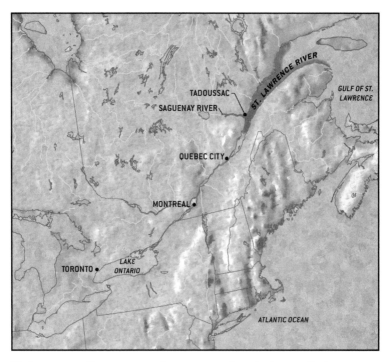

St. Lawrence shores support numerous chemical manufacturers. Some 25 potentially toxic compounds—including PCBs and DDT— have been found in belugas living in the river. Many whales are further laden with Mirex. The pesticide was made throughout the 1970s near Lake Ontario. Mirex contaminated eels that migrated down the St. Lawrence (*map*), where they were taken as food by the belugas. The whales stay near the mouth of the Saguenay in summer and spread out in winter.

examined 73 carcasses at the Faculty of Veterinary Medicine of the University of Montreal. Subsequent analyses confirmed that the entire population was highly contaminated with an array of chemicals. The salient pathological observations were stunning.

Forty percent of the animals bore tumors, 14 of which were cancerous, representing more than half of all malignancies ever reported in cetaceans. There was also a high incidence of stomach ulcers, including three cases of perforated ulcers, a condition never before documented in whales. Forty-five percent of the females produced only small amounts of milk because of infection, necrosis or tumors in their mammary glands. Lesions of the thyroid and adrenal glands were common. And many animals seemed to suffer from compromised immunity: a disproportionate number had opportunistic bacterial and protozoan infections; others had multisystemic diseases; and several had lost teeth. One whale we examined was a true hermaphrodite.

In comparison, other species of Arctic belugas did not display any of these conditions. Nor did other species of whales or seals living in the St. Lawrence. Both groups did, however, contain the same toxic substances as the belugas, albeit in lesser amounts. The maximum levels of PCBs in Arctic belugas were only some five parts per million (ppm), whereas St. Lawrence belugas had concentrations up to 100 times greater. Most tissue contained more than 50 ppm, which, according to Canadian regulations, made it toxic waste! We also discovered that the toxics were not confined to the fat in the blubber, as had been expected. Small amounts were found in the lipids present in other tissues, where they might have more readily injured vital organs.

III Effects of Organohalogens

Despite our findings, many marine biologists maintained that toxics were not at fault. They argued that even though the diseases and lesions we observed in the belugas matched the known effects of toxic chemicals, we had not yet demonstrated a cause-and-effect relationship. To do so, we had to single out a specific compound and the mechanism by which it might lead to disease. We turned our attention to the most striking disorder, cancer. Its incidence in the belugas was twice as high as in humans, higher than in horses and cats and only slightly lower than in dogs. If we restricted our comparison to cancers in the organs most often affected in whales—those of the gastrointestinal tract—the prevalence was more startling. It was exceeded only by that seen in sheep in Australia and New Zealand. There the high disease rate was attributed to treating pastures with carcinogenic herbicides.

We proposed that we had found a parallel situation of sorts. The sediments of the Saguenay contain tons of an extremely potent carcinogen, benzo(a)pyrene (BaP), which collects in invertebrates. For decades, one of the world's largest aluminum-producing complexes released BaP into the Saguenay.

We were able to demonstrate its presence in the belugas, but we were not certain how the BaP had entered their systems. The belugas are, however, unique among toothed whales in that in addition to eating fish, they dig into sediments to feed on bottom-dwelling invertebrates. Thus, it seemed reasonable to suggest that BaP had entered their systems in this way and had caused the higher rates of cancer found among the St. Lawrence belugas, ultimately contributing to their decreased numbers overall.

Industry officials, of course, disagreed with our suggestions, and, to be fair, the cancer data were confounding. A variety of organs—the stomach, intestine, bladder, salivary gland, liver, ovary and mammary gland—were affected. But exposure to a given carcinogen usually harms a specific tissue. So it seemed probable that other toxics might be at work. We looked first to organohalogens, the chemicals that were most abundant in the whales. Although they were not directly carcinogenic, there was evidence that they could disrupt the expression of certain genes. Also, in many animals, organohalogens impeded the activity of killer T cells, immune cells that ordinarily destroy malignant tumor cells.

Moreover, when given to experimental animals during embryonic, fetal and early postnatal stages, the chemicals caused defects in the nervous, endocrine and reproductive systems. They further stunted the production of needed immune proteins and immune cells. It was highly likely that organohalogens had such effects on whales, which would explain why the St. Lawrence belugas had been susceptible to various cancers and many other types of disease as well. Some lesions observed

Characteristics of Belugas

Beluga calves often travel with their mothers (*whales at right*). The calves are brown when born and gradually become gray and then white on reaching maturity. Adult female belugas are normally some 12 or 13 feet long; the larger males rarely attain 15 feet (*whale at left*). The whales communicate with one another and navigate the waters in which they live using a wide range of noises. They both focus and better receive these many sounds by changing the shape of their melon— a bulbous organ on their forehead. The calves receive nourishment solely from their mother's milk, which is some eight times richer than cow's milk. Among belugas in the St. Lawrence, the fats in this milk harbor high doses of toxics. Thus, successive generations of whales became more contaminated. —*P. B.*

among our samples indeed appeared to result from immunodeficiency.

Pathologist Sylvain De Guise, who had already autopsied dozens of the whales we found, joined a team directed by Michel Fournier at the University of Quebec in Montreal. This group was analyzing blood samples from live animals to count the types of immune cells present and to test whether these cells were functional. We decided to use similar methods to examine blood samples from the contaminated whales to look for a relation between the levels of organohalogens in the plasma and the numbers and response of immune cells.

First, we needed to describe the immune cells in a beluga's blood and adapt the tests to them. For this, we used blood samples from Arctic whales held captive at the Shedd Aquarium in Chicago and from wild ones that we momentarily restrained in their natural habitat. Then we adapted our analytical methods to measure minute amounts of toxics in the plasma. In cultures from Arctic beluga, we saw that their immune cells underwent changes when they were exposed to organohalogens in the laboratory. A recent study in the Netherlands also showed that captive seals suffered a suppression in immune function when fed naturally contaminated fish. The chemical levels in these fish were comparable to those in the St. Lawrence fish. We hope to get a definitive answer by sampling a number of live whales in the St. Lawrence in the near future.

We are particularly interested in determining the minimum levels at which the ill effects of organohalogens arise. All the whales and seals in the St. Lawrence system carry organohalogens to various degrees, but not all experience as much trouble as do the beluga. We know that the larger animals typically have lower levels of toxics. For instance, the smallest whale, the harbor porpoise, is the most contaminated, whereas the largest, the blue whale, is the least affected. The reason is that the smaller whale requires more food per pound of its body weight than does the larger whale. Moreover, the harbor porpoise takes fish from high in the food chain, where organohalogens accrete. The blue whale consumes base-level plankton.

Beluga whales are in fact far more contaminated than their size would indicate, which we originally found quite puzzling. Knowing the typical chemical contents in a pound of blubber, we estimated the total amount of each chemical within the entire population of 500 animals. Allowing for all the food they have taken in over 15 years, our model showed that the concentrations of toxics in local fish were much too low to account for the total burden we saw. So there was very likely another source.

We found that source by researching one particular chemical, called Mirex. We had been surprised earlier in the 1980s to find this insecticide—used against fire ants in the southern U.S.—in whales in eastern Canada. A follow-up study revealed that all the Mirex detected in the belugas was made at a chemical plant in New York State near Lake Ontario. It had seeped into the lake, where eels collected it in their tissues. Every October the adult eels migrated to the Atlantic to reproduce, first swimming down the St. Lawrence through the beluga habitat.

Turning back to our model, we found that if the belugas had fed on eels for only 10 days each year over the course of 15 years, they would have taken in the amounts of Mirex we were measuring in their tissues. The model also indicated that other chemicals in the eels—such as PCBs and DDT—explained half of the total organohalogen concentration seen in the whales. At this juncture, I felt like a naive detective who had been trying to figure out how packages move between cities by searching highway vehicles at random. I got nowhere until I chanced on a mail truck.

By the late 1980s the amount of organohalogens measured in Great Lakes fauna had decreased substantially. But we saw no similar reduction in the belugas. At first we assumed that perhaps improvements in the whales would occur only after some delay. They are, after all, removed from the Great Lakes, both geographically and in terms of the food chain. But eventually, an alternative explanation came to mind, and it does not bode very well for the future.

Up to 40 percent of the body weight of a beluga is blubber, and some 85 percent of that blubber is fat tissue, in which organohalogens concentrate. We noticed that organohalogen levels were often higher in very young animals than in older ones, contradicting the normal assumption that the toxics accumulated over the course of an animal's lifetime. We also found that the females were consistently less contaminated than the males. Taken together, these facts implied that the females passed significant amounts of chemicals on to their calves. We were able to prove the supposition by happening on a few females who had died shortly after giving birth. They were still producing milk, and it was some 35 percent fat. When tested, this fat held on average 10 ppm of PCBs, as well as other toxics.

Toxic Legacy of the St. Lawrence

The amount of toxics in the milk was only about a third of that normally found in the blubber of a female beluga. Still, it was an astounding amount—by human standards, anything containing more than 2 ppm of PCBs is considered unfit for consumption. It also meant that the toxics were transferred rapidly from mother to calf. The calf grows from about 50 kilograms at birth to 150 kilograms in one year by feeding on about four kilograms of milk each day. Assuming that the mother's blubber had 30 ppm of PCBs (and many adult females have more than three times that), that her milk fat had 10 ppm of PCBs and that roughly 70 percent of the PCBs were being passed on, over one year the mother would deliver to her calf about 3.8 grams of PCBs—translating into a concentration of 60 ppm in the blubber of the calf, or twice that found in the mother. All the while, the mother would consume 10 kilograms of fish a day, replenishing her own PCB load.

The milk provided the explanation. The suckling calf ingests food that is far more contaminated than its mother's food. In ecological terms, the calves feed at a higher echelon in the food chain, where the toxics have been further concentrated. Toxics first entered the St. Lawrence system in the 1930s and 1940s. We

Canaries of the Arctic Seas

Because belugas make an extraordinary range of noises—from whistles and creaks to clicks and warbles—the seafarers who first heard them named them sea canaries.

Although the number of belugas living in the St. Lawrence River has remained below 500 since the 1970s, experts estimate that some 100,000 belugas roam the Arctic seas around Alaska, Canada, Greenland, Scandinavia and Russia.

By tracking individual whales, scientists have learned that the whales often travel great distances, sometimes for several miles under the Arctic ice. In place of a dorsal fin, belugas sport a long ridge of fibrous tissue on their back. Using this ridge, they can break through several inches of ice to create a breathing hole.   —P. B.

have a sample of beluga blubber oil from the early 1950s that contains 5 ppm of PCBs. We now know that every new wave of calves started out with a blubber level of toxics above that of their mothers. They then took in fish that also contained progressively higher levels of toxics every year. So each new generation started from a less advantageous position than had the one before it.

This reasoning should apply to all predatory aquatic mammals, depending to some extent on their strategy regarding fat reserves and lactation. Lipids are a valuable substance—especially in cold seas—to be hoarded and passed on to the next generation. But when fats contain nonbiodegradable toxics, this legacy may be as poisonous as bad genes. In theory, the young animals should show more evidence of the acute effects of toxics in the St. Lawrence. But unfortunately, few belugas in their first years have been found.

In fact, we believe not many calves are being produced. The females, and perhaps the males as well, may not be as fertile as expected. The toxics they were exposed to in the womb could have stunted their reproductive development. And the toxics they ingest as adults could be disrupting hormonal cycles essential for reproduction. Some years ago it was shown that captive seals fed naturally contaminated fish did not produce offspring. The seals had low levels of vitamin A and its precursors—elements that are necessary for growth, reproduction and infection resistance.

Obviously, calving and maturing of the young to adulthood are the keys to a population's survival. Robert Michaud and Daniel Lefebvre of the St. Lawrence National Institute of Ecotoxicology spend months on the St. Lawrence every year, observing the lives of belugas. They conduct surveys from the air, estimating the sizes of herds and identifying their preferred habitats. They also work from a small boat, calculating the proportion of young whales. They have used photographs to identify more than 150 animals, several of whom are females with offspring of various ages. It is hoped in the years ahead that they will be resighted, giving us some measure of how often the females give birth and how many of these calves survive. Also, by following known whales, we can study the social structure of the population and, using skin biopsies as well, assess the degree of genetic relatedness in social groups.

We have no definite answers yet, but all the evidence indicates that the St. Lawrence belugas have failed to increase in number because of long-term exposure to a complex mixture of toxic chemicals. We have approached the problem from various angles and intend to pursue each one further. Studying whales anywhere requires a great deal of dedication. On the St. Lawrence, it also takes a strong heart and some degree of aloofness. Because we know many of the belugas individually, sailing among them is somewhat like visiting relatives. We do not find ourselves in foreign waters surrounded by swarms of whales as in the days of Jacques Cartier. They come to greet us in small groups, and we realize how important each one is for the future. We can afford to spend time with them, for there are no new lands to be discovered— only old ones to be understood and preserved, a task for which there is no one to guide us.

The Author

Pierre Béland is a senior research scientist at the St. Lawrence National Institute of Ecotoxicology. In this position—and previously as a research scientist for the Department of Fisheries and Oceans in Canada

*and as head of the Fisheries Ecology Research Center—
he has studied the marine ecosystems of the St. Lawrence
estuary and the Gulf of St. Lawrence. He has published
more than 60 scientific papers, 27 popular articles and
two books.*

4 Forging a Cleaner Future

The next article was written less than a year after the National Aeronautics and Space Administration (NASA) launched Terra, *its flagship earth-monitoring satellite. Today* Terra *circles the globe fourteen times each day, checking Earth's vital signs. Since it was launched,* Terra *has been capturing information on temperatures, clouds, and pollution with greater precision than has ever before been possible. On a day-to-day basis,* Terra *is helping scientists track the spread of pollutants and monitor air quality. The EPA, for example, is now using the satellite to track down the sources of aerosol and carbon monoxide pollution and to predict where the pollution will travel. Over the long run,* Terra *will provide scientists with a much clearer picture of how our climate is changing and how much of a role we are playing in that change.* Terra *is just one of sixteen satellites of the Earth Observing System (EOS) currently in orbit. Together they are providing scientists with the most extensive and accurate picture of Earth's climate in history. —SW*

"Monitoring Earth's Vital Signs"
by Michael D. King and David D. Herring
Scientific American, April 2000

Flying 705 kilometers above the earth's surface, a
satellite called Terra is conducting a comprehensive
health examination of our world. Everything from
clouds and plants to sunlight and temperature and fire
and ice influences climate, and Terra is just beginning
to collect this information every day over the entire
earth. As the bus-size satellite circles the globe from
pole to pole, its sensitive instruments track the planet's
vital signs as each region comes into view.

Certain environmental changes are occurring
today at rates never seen in our planet's recent history.
Imagine, for instance, the hundreds of fires set deliberately every year to clear land for agriculture, a practice
that has quadrupled during the past century. Humans
today burn an average of 142,000 square kilometers of
tropical forests—an area roughly the size of Arkansas—
every year. Some of Terra's sensors can track the flames
and gauge their intensity, whereas others measure the
extent of burn scars and observe how smoke particles
and gases move through the atmosphere. One of these
sensors can even distinguish changes at a resolution of
15 meters—a view close enough to pick out spots
where smoldering embers may again burst into flame.

Terra is the flagship of the Earth Observing
System (EOS), a National Aeronautics and Space
Administration satellite program that will bring

scientists closer to deciphering the earth's climate well enough to predict future changes—a charge that requires an unprecedented ability to differentiate natural cycles from changes that people create. Natural geologic forces, such as volcanic eruptions, variations in ocean currents and cycles of ice ages, have been rearranging the surface and climate of our planet since its formation 4.5 billion years ago. But today compelling scientific evidence illustrates that human activities are speeding up the rate of global change and have even attained the magnitude of a geologic force [see "The Human Impact on Climate," by Thomas R. Karl and Kevin E. Trenberth; SCIENTIFIC AMERICAN, December 1999].

We need to make many measurements all over the world, over a long period, in order to supply computer simulations with the right information to enable us to forecast climate change. To that end, we and our EOS colleagues identified 24 factors that together play a major role in determining climate. These factors include the flux of sunlight and other radiant energy, concentrations of greenhouse gases, snow and ice cover, clouds and aerosols, and changes in vegetation and other land-surface features. The Terra mission is designed to measure 16 of those 24 characteristics [*see list on page 161*].

In 1988 NASA's Earth System Sciences Committee issued a report calling for a long-term strategy for measuring the earth's vital signs. This committee emphasized that the only feasible way to monitor these signs consistently for a long time is by using satellite-borne sensors that can "see" the earth from space [see "Earth from Sky," by Diane L. Evans, Ellen R. Stofan, Thomas D. Jones and Linda M. Godwin; SCIENTIFIC AMERICAN, December 1994]. Consequently, in 1991, NASA initiated the Earth Observing System, and the U.S. Congress has since earmarked $7.4 billion to design and implement the program through October 2001. Our team devoted $1.3 billion to building and launching Terra, the newest member of the EOS fleet.

A New Generation of Remote Sensors

Terra rocketed into orbit on December 18, 1999, and specialists now guide its flight and control its sensors from a command center at the NASA Goddard Space Flight Center in Greenbelt, Md. Terra's sensors are not actively scanning the surface as do instruments that transmit laser or radar beams and track the way they bounce off the planet's surface. Terra's sensors are passive, much like a digital camera.

Packets of energy—sunlight and infrared light— escape the earth's atmosphere and pass through the sensors' apertures. Those energy packets then strike specially designed detectors that are sensitive to discrete wavelengths of electromagnetic energy. Similar to the way we can tune into different stations on a car radio, Terra's spectroradiometers enable researchers to detect different wavelengths of radiant energy. If those wavelengths are red, green and blue, they can easily make a color image that our eyes can see. If the measured

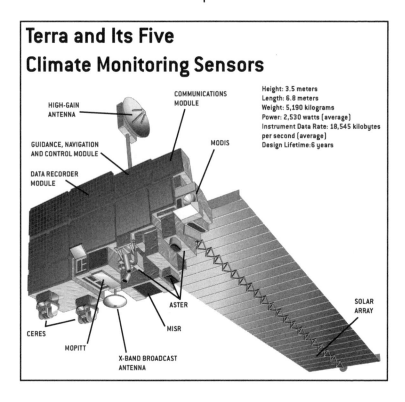

Terra and Its Five
Climate Monitoring Sensors

HIGH-GAIN
ANTENNA

COMMUNICATIONS
MODULE

GUIDANCE, NAVIGATION
AND CONTROL MODULE

MODIS

DATA RECORDER
MODULE

Height: 3.5 meters
Length: 6.8 meters
Weight: 5,190 kilograms
Power: 2,530 watts (average)
Instrument Data Rate: 18,545 kilobytes
per second (average)
Design Lifetime:6 years

SOLAR
ARRAY

CERES

ASTER

MISR

MOPITT

X-BAND BROADCAST
ANTENNA

wavelengths are invisible, such as those in the infrared
or ultraviolet portions of the spectrum, scientists must
assign them a visible color to make a "false-color" image
that our eyes can interpret.

The EOS missions rely on two integral components
in addition to the satellites: a system for storing the
information and people to interpret it. Already the
project supports some 850 scientists at government agencies and academic institutions around the world. What
the satellites beam back to the earth is a voluminous
stream of numbers—tens of trillions of bytes of information each week—that must be processed to become

Vital Signs That Terra Will Measure

 AEROSOLS

 AIR TEMPERATURE

 CLOUDS

 FIRES

 GLACIERS

 LAND TEMPERATURE

 LAND USE

 NATURAL DISASTERS

 OCEAN PRODUCTIVITY

 OCEAN TEMPERATURE

 POLLUTION

 RADIATION

 SEA ICE

 SNOW COVER

 VEGETATION

 WATER VAPOR

meaningful. An advanced computer network, called the EOS Data and Information System (EOSDIS), receives and processes the numbers. Four centers across the U.S. then archive the measurements from Terra and distribute them to scientists and civilians alike.

This free sharing of data contrasts sharply with many past satellite missions, for which public access was largely inaccessible to all but the highest-funded research organizations. A single image from the Landsat satellites, the first of which was launched in 1972, can cost hundreds or even thousands of dollars. Some of Terra's data, on the other hand, will be broadcast on X-band directly to anyone who has a compatible receiving station and the capacity to process and store such a huge flow of information. A variety of commercial markets can benefit from EOS data. Satellite maps of high productivity in the ocean, for instance, can guide commercial fishing outfits to likely concentrations of fish. In a similar fashion, images of agricultural fields will help farmers judge where crops are thriving and where they may be under stress. Such images can help farmers visualize patterns of runoff for particular fields and, in turn, refine their strategies for where, when and how much to irrigate and fertilize.

More Eyes in the Sky

In addition to Terra, three other EOS satellites are already orbiting the globe and measuring other vital signs of the climate, such as changes in the sun's energy output and winds blowing over the oceans. If these instruments survive their predicted lifetimes, and if Congress continues to fund the EOS effort, these satellites will be followed by 15 or more others, and together they will generate a 15-year global data set. To make accurate climate predictions, we will need such measurements spanning several decades.

Integrating observations from the sensors on board Terra and the other EOS satellites will make it possible to disentangle the myriad causes and effects that determine climate. Monitoring how patterns of deforestation correlate with rainfall and cloud cover, for example, will help researchers assess how the loss of trees affects regional water cycles. Comparing similar measurements from more than one sensor will help ensure that all instruments are seeing the same signals and that onboard calibration devices are working properly. Researchers will also compare the satellite measurements with those gleaned from dozens of other instruments based in aircraft, on ships and buoys, and on the ground.

continued on page 170

ASTER Advanced Spaceborne Thermal Emission and reflection Radiometer

Unique Characteristics: Highest spatial resolution of all Terra sensors and the unique ability to point toward special targets

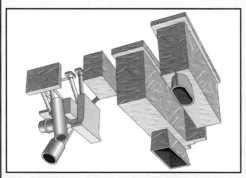

Sensors: Three distinct telescope subsystems that monitor wavelengths in the visible and near infrared, short-wave infrared, and thermal infrared portions of the spectrum

Vital Signs Measured:

Sponsor: Japanese Ministry of International Trade and Industry

Spatial Resolution: Ranging from 90 to 15 meters

The earth's land surfaces emit energy and temperatures that ASTER measures at ultrahigh resolution. These vital signs are key to estimating the planet's radiation budget and will be particularly useful for identifying rocks, soils and vegetation. Farmers can use such high-resolution, multispectral images to assess the way changes in surface temperature, ground slope and soil type impact the health of their crops. ASTER can also

continued on following page

continued from previous page

monitor ongoing changes in other surface features—such as receding glaciers and ice sheets, expanding desert boundaries, deforestation, floods and wildfires—which will help researchers distinguish between natural changes and those that humans cause. Because ASTER's telescopes can be tilted toward erupting volcanoes and other special targets, they can generate detailed stereoscopic images that will greatly refine digital topographic maps of the planet. These images will extend the collection that the Landsat satellites have been gathering since 1972.

CERES Clouds and the Earth's Radiant Energy System

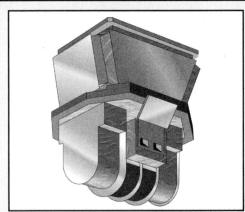

Unique Characteristic: **First satellite sensor to record radiation fluxes throughout the atmosphere**

Sensors: **Two broadband scanning radiometers**

Vital Signs Measured:

Sponsor: **NASA Langley Research Center**

Spatial Resolution: **20 kilometers**

Predicting global temperature change requires a keen understanding of how much radiation, in the form of heat and sunlight, enters and leaves the earth's atmosphere. Yet to date, researchers cannot account for about 8 percent of incoming solar radiation once it enters the atmosphere. One explanation for the missing energy is that clouds and aerosols—tiny particles of smoke and dust—absorb energy and scatter it in the lower atmosphere, where satellites that track the energy fluxes have never looked. To better quantify the roles that clouds play in the earth's energy system, CERES (with input from MODIS) will measure the flux of radiation twice as accurately as previous sensors, both at the top of the atmosphere and at the planet's surface. The CERES instruments extend the heritage begun by NASA's Earth Radiation Budget Experiment (ERBE) satellite sensors, which flew in the 1980s.

MOPITT Measurements Of Pollution In The Troposphere

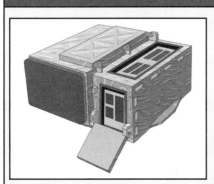

Unique Characteristic: First satellite sensor to trace pollutants to their source
Sensor: Scanning radiometer that uses gas correlation spectroscopy

continued on following page

continued from previous page

Vital Sign Measured: Sponsor: Canadian Space Agency
                         Spatial Resolution: 22 kilometers

Two trace gases won't escape MOPITT, which measures the global distribution and concentration of methane and carbon monoxide in the lower atmosphere. Methane—a greenhouse gas with nearly 30 times the heat-trapping capacity of carbon dioxide—is known to leak from swamps, livestock herds and icy deposits under the seafloor, but the output of these individual sources is not known. One way or another, methane is gathering in the lower atmosphere at a rate of about 1 percent a year. Carbon monoxide, which is expelled from factories, automobiles and forest fires, hinders the atmosphere's natural ability to rid itself of other harmful chemicals. The first satellite sensor to use gas correlation spectroscopy, MOPITT can distinguish these two gases from others, such as carbon dioxide and water vapor. As emitted heat or reflected sunlight enters the sensor, it passes through onboard containers of carbon monoxide and methane, producing a signal that correlates with the presence of these gases in the atmosphere.

MISR Multiangle Imaging SpectroRadiometer

Unique Characteristic: Produces stereoscopic images of clouds and smoke plumes
Sensors: Nine charge-coupled device (CCD) cameras

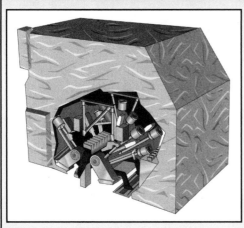

Sponsor: Jet Propulsion Laboratory

Spatial Resolution: **Ranging from 1.1 kilometers to 275 meters**

Vital Signs Measured:

No instrument like MISR has ever flown in space. Viewing the sunlit earth simultaneously at nine widely spaced angles, MISR collects global images of reflected sunlight in four colors (blue, green, red and near-infrared).The way the reflections change from one view angle to another will make it possible to distinguish different types of clouds, aerosols and land surfaces. Researchers can combine MISR images with stereoscopic techniques to design three-dimensional models that will help them trace aerosols and smoke plumes back to their sources. And as MISR covers the globe at the equator once every nine days, its multiangle measurements will enable researchers to better interpret the roles that clouds and aerosols play in the planet's energy budget.

MODIS MODerate-resolution Imaging Spectroradiometer

Unique Characteristic: Only Terra sensor to see the entire planet's surface every one to two days

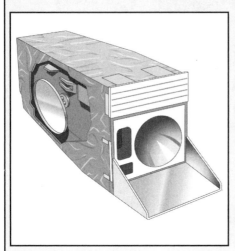

Sensors: Four sets of detectors that are sensitive to visible light and to radiation in the near, shortwave, midwave and thermal portions of the infrared spectrum

Sponsor: NASA Goddard Space Flight Center

Vital Signs Measured:

Spatial Resolution: Ranging from 1 kilometer to 250 meters

Seeing the entire globe in 36 discrete spectral bands, MODIS tracks a wider array of the earth's vital signs than any other Terra sensor. For instance, the sensor measures the percentage of the planet's surface that is covered by clouds almost every day with its sweeping 2,330-kilometer-wide viewing swath. This wide spatial coverage will enable MODIS, together with MISR and CERES, to determine the impact of clouds on the planet's energy budget—an important contribution considering that clouds remain the greatest area of uncertainty in global climate models. The sensor has an unprecedented channel (centered at 1.375 microns) for detection of wispy cirrus clouds that are believed to contribute to global warming by trapping heat emitted from the surface. MODIS will also monitor how smoke plumes and other aerosols mingle with clouds and alter their ability to absorb and reflect energy.

As it monitors global cloud cover, MODIS will also help investigators track changes to the land surface. The sensor is mapping the extent of snow and ice brought by winter storms and frigid temperatures, and it will observe the "green wave" sweep across continents as winter gives way to spring and vegetation blooms in response. It will see where and when disasters strike—such as volcanic eruptions, floods, severe storms, droughts and wildfires—and will help guide people out of harm's way. MODIS's bands are particularly sensitive to fires; they can distinguish flaming from smoldering burns and provide better estimates of the amounts of aerosols and gases they release into the atmosphere.

The sensor is also ideal for monitoring large-scale changes in the biosphere that will yield new insights into

continued on following page

continued from previous page

the workings of the global carbon cycle. Although no current satellite sensor can measure directly carbon dioxide concentrations in the atmosphere, MODIS can quantify the photosynthetic activity of plants to estimate how much of the greenhouse gas they are absorbing. In addition, the sensor will take a sophisticated look at the marine biosphere by measuring the fluorescent glow of chlorophyll in the ocean.

continued from page 162

The process of diagnosing climate takes hundreds of hours of computer time. The first four-dimensional "snapshot" of our planet will probably not be ready until next winter, and scientists may need many years after that to complete the first thorough statistical evaluation. The earth's climate system is intricately interconnected. What we have described here only scratches the surface of what the Terra mission can accomplish. Many of its contributions will undoubtedly prove to be serendipitous as innovative studies and new applications emerge in the years ahead.

The Authors

Michael D. King is the senior project scientist of the National Aeronautics and Space Administration's Earth Observing System (EOS). From a command center at the NASA Goddard Space Flight Center in Greenbelt, Md., King supports hundreds of scientists worldwide who use

EOS satellites to study global climate change. King joined the Goddard staff in 1978 as a physical scientist in the Laboratory for Atmospheres. Science writer David D. Herring works under contract for the EOS project and spearheads the team that promotes the Terra satellite to the public.

For more than two decades, Harvard University professor Joel Schwartz has been contending that tiny particles in the air we breathe could be hazardous to our health. These particles, which are made up of things like dust, dirt, soot, smoke, and chemicals released by industries, cars, and power plants, can get inside our lungs and cause serious health problems. Schwartz has shown in studies how death rates in communities swing up and down in sync with rising and falling concentrations of particulate matter in the air. As this article indicates, his findings have not made him popular with industry leaders. But he remains undeterred in his efforts. His research was instrumental in setting the current particulate matter standards, which apply to fine particles 2.5 microns or less in diameter. But scientists at the EPA are now pushing to tighten air quality standards even further to include larger particulate matter in their regulations. —SW

"Where the Bodies Lie"
by Gary Stix
Scientific American, June 1998

Joel Schwartz is the antithesis of the epidemiologist as public accountant of the medical profession—the cautious record keeper who never goes beyond highly qualified statements about plausible statistical association between pollutant exposure and disease. His method of employing high-powered statistical techniques to find ties between fine combustion particles and premature deaths is coupled with an activist's sensibility. "If you think that all a public health professional should do is to publish papers and pad a CV, then you should get another job," Schwartz says.

Schwartz is one of the scientists most closely associated with the research that led to new Environmental Protection Agency regulations last year to reduce levels of microscopic particles measuring 2.5 microns in diameter or less. These "fine" particles are by-products of combustion from industrial plants, woodstoves and motor vehicles. During the multiyear debate over new rules, the outspoken qualities of the tall, intense figure with the salt-and-pepper beard made him a lightning rod for industry officials who have attacked particulate research as "junk science."

Schwartz's influence, though, relates as much to his technical prowess as to his advocacy. "As the industry started to look at Joel's work and hire their own analysts, it took a while for them to catch up with the sophistication of his statistical analysis," says Daniel

Greenbaum, president of the Health Effects Institute, an independent nonprofit group funded by the EPA and industry.

The 50-year-old Schwartz was among a small group of air-pollution researchers during the late 1980s who began to make extensive use of time-series analysis—the examination of how one variable changes in relation to another over time. Time series had been used by econometricians to track inflation or gross national product but was not widely deployed in studying air pollution. These techniques—combined with methods of accounting for nonlinear effects, such as the sharp rise in deaths at temperature extremes—allow one to track sickness and mortality from one day to another as air-pollution levels rise and fall. Using time series, a researcher can discard a host of confounding variables, such as whether a patient was a smoker or had high blood pressure. The amount a person smokes from day to day is unlikely to be correlated with changes in particulate air pollution.

Excluding details such as smoking greatly simplifies the process of obtaining data. A researcher can seek out death certificates, hospital admissions and other readily available public records without having to look for recruits for a multimillion-dollar study. "It makes things cheap," Schwartz says. "All you need is a little money to pay a salary while you're crunching numbers." In the early 1990s Schwartz cranked out a wad of these studies that showed associations between relatively low levels of particulates and death or illness from respiratory or cardiovascular ailments in city after city across the U.S. More recently, he has served as a collaborator on similar studies conducted across Europe.

The innovative qualities that Schwartz brings to his labors may result from his training as a theoretical solid-state physicist and mathematician, not an epidemiologist. "The culture of physics is much more adventurous than the culture of medicine, where you don't want to kill patients," Schwartz says. "In physics, the faster you get out flaky ideas, the faster you find out which ones are right and which ones are wrong." When Schwartz left Brandeis University in the mid-1970s, however, he could not find a job as a physicist. After serving as a congressional aide, he moved to the policy office of the EPA in 1979 as an energy economist.

Schwartz made his mark in the early 1980s at the agency when the Reagan administration tried to halt the phase-out of lead in gasoline as part of a larger regulatory reform effort. His supervisors asked him to produce a study to show the savings to industry once the rules on scaling back of lead were eliminated. "I did it, and then I asked what was the other side of the coin," he says. On his own, Schwartz then undertook an analysis that revealed that the $100 million or so savings to industry would be more than offset by health costs that could total more than $1 billion annually. His study helped to convince the agency to reverse its position and actually tighten standards. In 1985, working with his wife, Ronnie Levin, another EPA scientist, Schwartz completed a new cost-benefit study that bolstered the case for additional rules that resulted in totally eliminating lead from gasoline. "Schwartz's

STANDARDS FOR PARTICULATE MATTER (MICROGRAMS PER CUBIC METER OF AIR)	1987 STANDARD	1997 STANDARD
≤10-MICRON-DIAMETER PARTICLES		
24-HOUR AVERAGE	150	150
ANNUAL AVERAGE	50	50
≤2.5-MICRON-DIAMETER PARTICLES		
24-HOUR AVERAGE	NONE	65
ANNUAL AVERAGE	NONE	15

work clearly delineated how much people were paying in terms of monetized health costs; it was a revolution to put those things into the thinking about lead," says Herbert Needleman, a University of Pittsburgh professor who is a prominent researcher on health effects of lead.

During the mid-1980s, Schwartz began to fashion a job description for himself as an epidemiologist with a focus on air pollution. He consciously avoided Superfund and the other hazardous-waste issues that occupied many of the agency's resources. "Even if something's going on with hazardous wastes, the number of cases is not going to be very large in terms of the overall public health impact," he says. "It's not where the bodies lie. I view myself as exploring places missed where the overall public health impact is likely to be large."

In 1986 he reassessed a 14-year-long study of air pollution and health data in London. Particulates—not sulfur dioxide—seemed to be linked to early deaths and illness. Schwartz's analysis aided in fashioning a 1987 standard that set a daily and annual average for particulate matter with a diameter of 10 microns or less, called PM 10. But he felt the standard did not suffice, because his investigation had shown that there was no detectable threshold at which people stopped becoming sick. The EPA rule failed to target the smallest particles produced by combustion from power plants, trucks and other sources. So Schwartz plowed on: "I kept turning out studies using U.S. data until people couldn't ignore it anymore."

In 1991 Schwartz's work on lead and particles resulted in his becoming a MacArthur Fellow. Schwartz was the first federal career employee to receive the so-called genius award—an event that prompted EPA administrator William Reilly to remark: "Every time you fill up your car with gasoline, you can think of Joel Schwartz."

The MacArthur Award also provided him with an escape route from his cramped, windowless office at the EPA. "It was clear that the PM [particulate matter] stuff was getting very hot," Schwartz says. "If I had still been a federal employee, I would have been harassed to death." The $275,000, no strings-attached grant allowed him to take a slight pay cut for an associate professor's job at the Harvard School of Public Health and to afford a home in the Boston area.

Schwartz's expectations about the coming fight over particulates were amply fulfilled. In the several years leading up to the new rules, Schwartz and his colleagues Douglas Dockery of Harvard and C. Arden Pope III of Brigham Young University saw their studies subjected to an onslaught of attacks, often from industry-funded scientists.

One pointed critique came from Suresh Moolgavkar, a University of Washington professor whose investigations were paid for by the American Iron and Steel Institute. Moolgavkar's findings showed that reported links to higher death rates cannot be attributed to particulates alone. Sulfur dioxide, carbon monoxide, ozone and other pollutants may have also contributed to the mortality. Schwartz responds that similar ties between premature death and particulates can be found in cities where one or more of the other confounding pollutants are present at low levels.

The debate's shrillness picked up last year, when Harvard researchers were lambasted for refusing to release to outside scientists raw data from their "Six Cities Study," a widely cited report that found a link between particulates and death rates over a 16-year period. Dockery, the lead researcher, refused because of confidentiality agreements with study subjects. He also expressed an aversion to letting critics pick apart the data. The data were subsequently provided to the Health Effects Institute for reanalysis. Not, however, before Schwartz was quoted in the *Wall Street Journal* defending the study team against scientists he called "industry thugs."

Although the EPA promulgated the new rules last July for ozone as well as 2.5-micron particles, the controversy surrounding the issue means that the policy firestorm will most likely continue. The agency is treading cautiously, taking several years to conduct particle monitoring and scientific studies before states are required to submit implementation plans. The rules, in fact, allow states to take well over a decade to come into full compliance, much to Schwartz's chagrin. "We're going to postpone public health for 14 years," he says. "Meanwhile people are going to die."

Schwartz's pace has not slackened, however. An article he published with his wife and another researcher in the November issue of the journal *Epidemiology* used a time-series analysis that found a relation between the turbidity (cloudiness) of filtered drinking water—a possible indicator of microbial contamination—and emergency visits and admissions for gastrointestinal complaints to a Philadelphia hospital. "I'm getting in trouble in another area," he notes, commenting on an attack from water utilities that came after the article was published.

At times, Schwartz worries that his bluntness may affect support for his endeavors: "I think industry is trying to compromise my ability to get more money to do research, and I think there's a risk they'll succeed." But Schwartz is unlikely to muzzle himself. "When I look at the statistics, I see more people dying of particle air pollution than are dying of AIDS, and I need to call that to people's attention," he says.

In the classic cartoon show The Jetsons, *which originally premiered on the ABC television network in 1962, cars fly around floating cities on aerial freeways. We now know that the 1960s vision of twenty-first-century transportation was eons away from reality. Today, our visions of future transportation are far more realistic and practical. With the environment in jeopardy, we are in search of a car that will be efficient, cost-effective, and have low emissions. What will fuel this vehicle of tomorrow?*

Author Matthew L. Wald ponders the potential of one contender: the hydrogen fuel cell. As he points out, this technology has several obstacles to overcome, but it has not yet been knocked out of the ring. The reality of a hydrogen economy may actually be closer than we had imagined. Nine European cities have introduced hydrogen fuel cell buses into their public transportation systems. In the summer of 2005, a family in California became the first in the United States to lease a hydrogen-powered car—the Honda FCX. General Motors plans to make fuel cell vehicles a commercial reality, putting 1 million of its "hydro" cars on the road within the next decade. —SW

"Questions About a Hydrogen Economy"
by Matthew L. Wald
Scientific American, May 2004

In the fall of 2003, a few months after President George W. Bush announced a $1.7-billion research program to

develop a vehicle that would make the air cleaner and
the country less dependent on imported oil, Toyota
came to Washington, D.C., with two of them. One, a
commercially available hybrid sedan, had a conventional, gasoline-fueled internal-combustion engine
supplemented by a battery-powered electric motor. It
got about 50 miles to the gallon, and its carbon dioxide
emissions were just over half those of an average car.
The other auto, an experimental SUV, drove its electric
motor with hydrogen fuel cells and emitted as waste
only water purer than Perrier and some heat. Which
was cleaner?

Answering that question correctly could have a big
impact on research spending, on what vehicles the
government decides to subsidize as it tries to incubate
a technology that will wean us away from gasoline
and, ultimately, on the environment. But the answer is
not what many people would expect, at least according
to Robert Wimmer, research manager for technical
and regulatory affairs at Toyota. He said that the two
vehicles were about the same.

Wimmer and an increasing number of other experts
are looking beyond simple vehicle emissions, to the total
effect on the environment caused by the production of
the vehicle's fuel and its operation combined. Seen in a
broader context, even the supposed great advantages of
hydrogen, such as the efficiency and cleanliness of fuel
cells, are not as overwhelming as might be thought.
From this perspective, coming in neck and neck with a
hybrid is something of an achievement; in some cases,

Overview/*Hydrogen Economy*

- Per a given equivalent unit of fuel, hydrogen fuel cells in vehicles are about twice as efficient as internal-combustion engines. Unlike conventional engines, fuel cells emit only water vapor and heat.
- Hydrogen doesn't exist freely in nature, however, so producing it depends on current energy sources. Sources of hydrogen are either expensive and not widely available (including electrolysis using renewables such as solar, wind or hydropower), or else they produce undesirable greenhouse gases (coal or other fossil fuels).
- Ultimately hydrogen may not be the universal cure-all, although it may be appropriate for certain applications. Transportation may not be one of them.

the fuel-cell car can be responsible for substantially more carbon dioxide emissions, as well as a variety of other pollutants, the Department of Energy states. And in one way the hybrid is, arguably, superior: it already exists as a commercial product and thus is available to cut pollution now. Fuel-cell cars, in contrast, are expected on about the same schedule as NASA's manned trip to Mars and have about the same level of likelihood.

If that sounds surprising, it is also revealing about the uncertainties and challenges that trail the quest for a hydrogen economy—wherein most energy is devoted to the creation of hydrogen, which is then run through a fuel cell to make electricity. Much hope surrounds the advances in fuel cells and the possibility of a cleaner hydrogen economy, which could include not only transportation but also power for houses and other buildings. Last November U.S. Energy Secretary Spencer Abraham told a Washington gathering of energy ministers from 14 countries and the European Union that hydrogen could "revolutionize the world in which we live." Noting that the nation's more than 200 million motor vehicles consume about two thirds of the 20 million barrels of oil the U.S. uses every day, President Bush has called hydrogen the "freedom fuel."

But hydrogen is not free, in either dollars or environmental damage. The hydrogen fuel cell costs nearly 100 times as much per unit of power produced as an internal-combustion engine. To be price competitive, "you've got to be at a nickel a watt, and we're at $4 a watt," says Tim R. Dawsey, a research associate at Eastman Chemical Company, which makes polymers for fuel cells. Hydrogen is also about five times as expensive, per unit of usable energy, as gasoline. Simple dollars are only one speed bump on the road to the hydrogen economy. Another is that supplying the energy required to make pure hydrogen may itself cause pollution. Even if that energy is from a renewable source, like the sun or the wind, it may have more environmentally sound uses than the production of hydrogen. Distribution and storage of hydrogen—the least dense gas in the universe—are other technological and infrastructure difficulties. So is the safe handling of the gas. Any practical proposal for a hydrogen economy will have to address all these issues.

Which Sources Make Sense?

Hydrogen fuel cells have two obvious attractions. First, they produce no pollution at point of use [see "Vehicle of Change," by Lawrence D. Burns, J. Byron McCormick and Christopher E. Borroni-Bird; SCIENTIFIC AMERICAN, October 2002]. Second, hydrogen can come from myriad sources. In fact, the gas is not a fuel in the conventional sense. A fuel is something found in nature, like coal, or refined from a natural product, like diesel fuel from oil, and then burned to do work. Pure hydrogen does not exist naturally on earth and is so highly processed that it is really more of a carrier or medium for storing and transporting energy from some original source to a machine that makes electricity. "The beauty of hydrogen is the fuel diversity that's possible," said David K. Garman, U.S. assistant secretary for energy efficiency and renewable energy. Each source, however, has an ugly side.

For instance, a process called electrolysis makes hydrogen by splitting a water molecule with electricity [*see illustration on page 193*]. The electricity could come from solar cells, windmills, hydropower or safer, next-generation nuclear reactors [see "Next-Generation Nuclear Power," by James A. Lake, Ralph G. Bennett and John F. Kotek; SCIENTIFIC AMERICAN, January 2002]. Researchers are also trying to use microbes to transform biomass, including parts of crops that now have no economic value, into hydrogen. In February researchers at the University of Minnesota and the University of Patras in Greece announced a chemical reactor that generates hydrogen from ethanol mixed with water. Though appealing, all these technologies are either unaffordable or unavailable on a commercial scale and are likely to remain so for many years to come, according to experts.

Hydrogen could be derived from coal-fired electricity, which is the cheapest source of energy in most parts of the country. Critics argue, though, that if coal is the first ingredient for the hydrogen economy, global warming could be exacerbated through greater release of carbon dioxide.

Or hydrogen could come from the methane in natural gas, methanol or other hydrocarbon fuel [*see illustration on page 193*]. Natural gas can be reacted with steam to make hydrogen and carbon dioxide. Filling fuel cells, however, would preclude the use of natural gas for its best industrial purpose today: burning in high-efficiency combined-cycle turbines to generate electricity. That, in turn, might again lead to more coal use. Combined-cycle plants can turn 60 percent of the heat of burning natural gas into electricity; a coal plant converts only about 33 percent. Also, when burned, natural gas produces just over half as much carbon dioxide per unit of heat as coal does, 117 pounds per million Btu versus 212. As a result, a kilowatt-hour of electricity made from a new natural gas plant has slightly over one fourth as much carbon dioxide as a kilowatt-hour from coal. (Gasoline comes between coal and natural gas, at 157 pounds of carbon dioxide per million Btu.) In sum, it seems better for the environment to use natural gas to make electricity for the grid and save coal, rather than turning it into hydrogen to save gasoline.

Two other fuels could be steam-reformed to give off hydrogen: the oil shipped from Venezuela or the Persian Gulf and, again, the coal from Appalachian mines. To make hydrogen from fossil fuels in a way that does not add to the release of climate-changing carbon dioxide, the carbon must be captured so that it does not enter the atmosphere. Presumably this process would be easier than sequestering carbon from millions of tailpipes. Otherwise, the fuels might as well be burned directly.

"If you look at it from the whole system, not the individual sector, you may do better to get rid of your coal-fired power plants, because coal is such a carbon-intensive fuel," says Michael Wang, an energy researcher at Argonne National Laboratory. Coal accounts for a little more than half the kilowatt-hours produced in the U.S.; about 20 percent is from natural gas. The rest comes from mostly carbon-free sources, primarily nuclear reactors and hydroelectricity. Thus, an effort to replace the coal-fired electric plants would most likely take decades.

In any case, if hydrogen were to increase suddenly in supply, fuel cells might not even be the best use for the gas. In a recent paper, Reuel Shinnar, professor of chemical engineering at the City College of New York, reviewed the alternatives for power and fuel production. Rather than the use of hydrogen as fuel, he suggested something far simpler: increased use of hydrocracking and hydrotreating. The U.S. could save three million barrels of oil a day that way, Shinnar calculated. Hydrocracking and hydrotreating both start with molecules in crude oil that are unsuitable for gasoline because they are too big and have a carbon-to-hydrogen ratio that is too heavy with carbon. The processes are expensive but still profitable, because they allow the refineries to take ingredients that are good for only low-value products, such as asphalt and boiler fuel, and turn them into gasoline. It is like turning chuck steak into sirloin.

What About Conversion Costs?

If hydrogen production is dirty and expensive, could its impressive energy efficiency at point of use make up for those downsides? Again, the answer is complicated.

A kilo of hydrogen contains about the same energy as a gallon of unleaded regular gas—that is, if burned, each would give off about the same amount of heat. But the internal-combustion engine and the fuel cell differ in their ability to extract usable work from that fuel energy. In the engine, most of the energy flows out of the tailpipe as heat, and additional energy is lost to friction inside the engine. In round numbers, advocates and detractors agree, a fuel cell gets twice as much

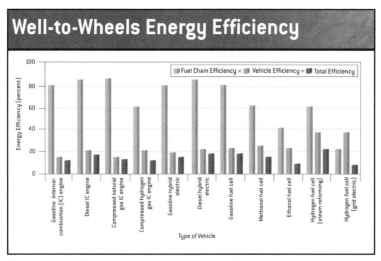

Well-to-Wheels Energy Efficiency

Total energy efficiency includes not only vehicle operation but also the energy required to produce fuel. Extracting oil, refining gasoline and trucking that fuel to filling stations for internal-combustion engines is more efficient than creating hydrogen for fuel cells.

work out of a kilo of hydrogen as an engine gets out of a gallon of gas. (In a stationary application—such as a basement appliance that takes the hydrogen from natural gas and turns it into electricity to run the household—efficiency could be higher, because the heat given off by the fuel-cell process could also be used—for example, to heat tap water.)

There is, in fact, a systematic way to evaluate where best to use each fuel. A new genre of energy analysis, "well to wheels," compares the energy efficiency of every known method to turn a vehicle's wheels [*see illustration above*]. The building block of the well-to-wheels performance is "conversion efficiency." At every step of the energy chain, from pumping oil out of the ground to refining it to burning it in an engine, some of the original energy potential of the fuel is lost.

The first part of the well-to-wheels determination is what engineers call "well to tank": what it takes to make and deliver a fuel. When natural gas is cracked for hydrogen, about 40 percent of the original energy potential is lost in the transfer, according to the DOE Office of Energy Efficiency and Renewable Energy. Using electricity from the grid to make hydrogen by electrolysis of water causes a loss of 78 percent. (Despite the lower efficiency of electrolysis, it is likely to predominate in the early stages of a hydrogen economy because it is convenient—producing the hydrogen where it is needed and thus avoiding shipping problems.) In contrast, pumping a gallon of oil out of the ground, taking it to a refinery, turning it into gasoline and getting that petrol to a filling station loses about 21 percent of the energy potential. Producing natural gas and compressing it in a tank loses only about 15 percent.

The second part of the total energy analysis is "tank to wheels," or the fraction of the energy value in the vehicle's tank that actually ends up driving the wheels. For the conventional gasoline internal-combustion engine, 85 percent of the energy in the gasoline tank is lost; thus, the whole system, well to tank combined with tank to wheels, accounts for a total loss of 88 percent.

The fuel cell converts about 37 percent of the hydrogen's energy value to power for the wheels. The total loss, well to wheels, is about 78 percent if the hydrogen comes from steam-reformed natural gas. If the source of the hydrogen is electrolysis from coal, the loss from the well (a mine, actually) to tank is 78 percent; after that hydrogen runs through a fuel cell, it loses another 43 percent, with the total loss reaching 92 percent.

Wally Rippel, a research engineer at AeroVironment in Monrovia, Calif., who helped to develop the General Motors EV-1 electric car and the NASA Helios Solar Electric airplane, offers another way to look at the situation. He calculates that in a car that employs an electric motor to turn the wheels, a kilowatt-hour used to recharge batteries will propel the auto three times as far as if that same kilowatt-hour were instead used to make hydrogen for a fuel cell.

All these facts add up to an argument *not* to use electricity to make hydrogen and then go back to electricity again with an under-the-hood fuel cell. But there is one strong reason to go through inefficient multiple conversions. They may still make economic sense, and money is what has shaped the energy markets so far. That is, even if the hydrogen system is very wasteful of energy, there are such huge differences in the cost of energy from various sources that it might make sense to switch to a system that lets us go where the cheapest energy is.

Walter "Chip" Schroeder, president and chief executive of Proton Energy Systems, a Connecticut company that builds electrolysis machines, explains the economic logic. Coal at current prices (which is to

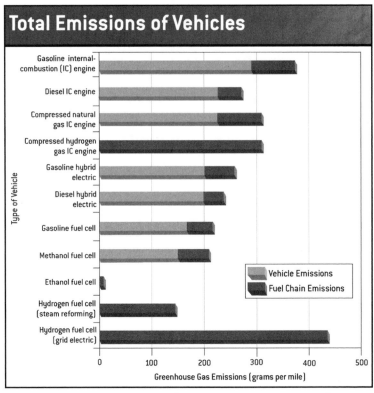

Total Emissions of Vehicles

Emissions of greenhouse gases (carbon dioxide or equivalent) vary depending on the combined effects of the vehicle's operation and the source of the fuel. Fuel-cell vehicles emit no greenhouse gases themselves, but the creation of the hydrogen fuel can be responsible for more emissions overall than conventional gasoline internal-combustion engines are. (The Energy Department calculates that ethanol derived from corn has almost no greenhouse gas emission, because carbon emitted by ethanol use is reabsorbed by new corn.)

say, coal at prices that are likely to prevail for years to come) costs a little more than 80 cents per million Btu. Gasoline at $1.75 a gallon (which seems pricey at the moment but in a few months or years could look cheap) is about $15.40. The mechanism for turning a Btu from coal into a Btu that will run a car is cumbersome, but in the transition, "you end up with wine, not water," he says. Likewise, he describes his device to turn water into hydrogen as an "arbitrage machine." "Arbitrage" is the term used by investment bankers or stock or commodities traders to describe buying low and selling high, but it usually refers to small differences in the price of a stock or the value of a currency between one market or another. "You can't make reasonable policy without understanding just how extreme the value differentials in our energy marketplace are," Schroeder says.

How to Deliver the Hydrogen?

Different sources of energy may not be as fungible as money is in arbitrage, however. There is a problem making hydrogen conveniently available at a good cost, at least if the hydrogen is going to come from renewable sources such as solar, hydropower or wind that are practical in only certain areas of the country.

Hydrogen from wind, for example, is competitive with gasoline when wind power costs three cents a kilowatt-hour, says Garman of the DOE. That occurs where winds blow steadily. "Where I might get three-cent wind tends to be in places where people don't live," he notes. In the U.S., such winds exist in a belt running from Montana and the Dakotas to Texas. The electric power they produce would have a long way to go to reach the end users—with energy losses throughout the grid along the way. "You can't get the electrons out of the Dakotas because of transmission constraints," Garman points out. "Maybe a hydrogen pipeline could get the tremendous wind resource carried to Chicago," the nearest motor-fuel market.

That is, if such a pipeline were even practical to build. Given hydrogen's low density, it is far harder to deliver than, for instance, natural gas. To move large volumes of any gas requires compressing it, or else the pipeline has to have a diameter similar to that of an airplane fuselage. Compression takes work, and that drains still more energy from the total production process. Even in this instance, managing hydrogen is trickier than dealing with other fuel gases. Hydrogen compressed to about 790 atmospheres has less than a third of the energy of the methane in natural gas at the same pressure, points out a recent study by three European researchers, Ulf Bossel, Baldur Eliasson and Gordon Taylor.

A related problem is that a truck that could deliver 2,400 kilos of natural gas to a user would yield only 288 kilos of hydrogen pressurized to the same level, Bossel and his colleagues find. Put another way, it would take about 15 trucks to deliver the hydrogen needed to power the same number of cars that could be served by a single gasoline tanker. Switch to liquid hydrogen, and it would take only about three trucks to equal the one gasoline tanker, but hydrogen requires substantially more effort to liquefy. Shipping the hydrogen as methanol that could be reformed onboard

Creating Hydrogen

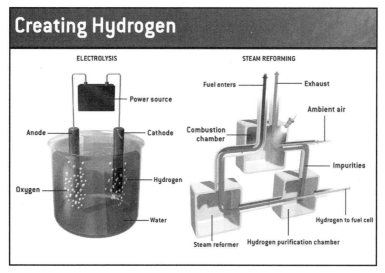

Two main methods are known for extracting hydrogen, which does not occur in pure form naturally on the earth. Electrolysis (*left*) uses electric current to split molecules of water (H_2O). A cathode (negative terminal) attracts hydrogen atoms, and an anode (positive) attracts oxygen; the two gases bubble up into air and can be captured. In steam reforming (*right*), a hydro-carbon such as methanol (CH_3OH) first vaporizes in a heated combustion chamber. A catalyst in the steam reformer breaks apart fuel and water vapor to produce components including hydrogen, which is then separated and routed to a fuel cell.

the vehicle [*see illustration above*] would ease transport, but again, the added transition has an energy penalty. These facts argue for using the hydrogen where it is produced, which may be distant from the major motor-fuel markets.

No matter how hydrogen reaches its destination, the difficulties of handling the elusive gas will not be over. Among hydrogen's disadvantages is that it burns readily. All gaseous fuels have a minimum and maximum concentration at which they will burn. Hydrogen's range is unusually broad, from 2 to 75 percent. Natural gas, in contrast, burns between 5 and 15 percent. Thus, as dangerous as a leak of natural gas is, a hydrogen leak is worse, because hydrogen will ignite at a wider range of concentrations. The minimum energy necessary to ignite hydrogen is also far smaller than that for natural gas.

And when hydrogen burns, it does so invisibly. NASA published a safety manual that recommends checking for hydrogen fires by holding a broom at arm's length and seeing if the straw ignites. "It's scary—you cannot see the flame," says Michael D. Amiridis, chair of the department of chemical engineering at the University of South Carolina, which performs fuel-cell research under contract for a variety of companies. A successful fuel-cell car, he says, would have "safety standards at least equivalent to the one I have now." A major part of the early work on developing a hydrogen fueling supply chain has been building warning instruments that can reliably detect hydrogen gas.

A Role for Hydrogen

Despite the technological and infrastructure obstacles, a hydrogen economy may be coming. If it is, it will most likely resemble the perfume economy, a market where quantities are so small that unit prices do not matter. Chances are good that it will start in cellular phones and laptop computers, where consumers might

Same Hydrogen, Different Volumes

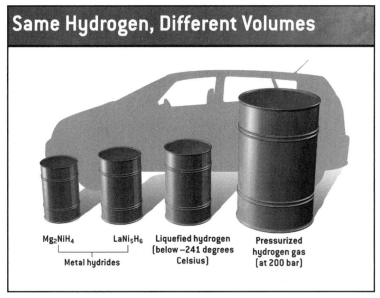

| Mg_2NiH_4 | $LaNi_5H_6$ | Liquefied hydrogen (below −241 degrees Celsius) | Pressurized hydrogen gas (at 200 bar) |

Metal hydrides

Containing the lightest gas in the universe onboard a car presents a challenge, as is clear from the differences in volume of some options for storing four kilograms of hydrogen—enough for a 250-mile driving range. (Four kilograms of hydrogen holds about the same energy as four gallons of gasoline. Because fuel cells are about twice as efficient as internal-combustion engines, that four kilograms takes the car as far as eight gallons of gasoline.) Current alternatives, including tanks that hold pressurized gas or liquefied hydrogen, are too big. Experimental metal hydrides or other solid-state technologies might be able to release hydrogen on demand and be recharged later, but they also carry a weight penalty or an energy penalty for the chemical transformations.

not mind paying $10 a kilowatt-hour for electricity from fuel cells; a recent study by the fuel-cell industry predicts that the devices could be sold in laptop computers this year. It might eventually move to houses, which will run nicely on five kilowatts or so and where an improvement in carbon efficiency is highly desirable because significant electricity demand exists almost every hour of the day. But hydrogen cells may not appear in great numbers in driveways, where cars have a total energy requirement of about 50 kilowatts apiece but may run only an average of two hours a day—a situation that is exactly backward from where a good engineer would put a device like a fuel cell, which has a low operating cost but a high cost per unit of capacity. Although most people may have heard of fuel cells as alternative power sources for cars, cars may be the last place they'll end up on a commercial scale.

If we need to find substitutes for oil for transportation, we may look to several places before hydrogen. One is natural gas, with very few technical details to work out and significant supplies available. Another is electricity for electric cars. Battery technology has hit some very significant hurdles, but they might be easier to solve than those of fuel cells. If we have to, we can run vehicles on methanol from coal; the Germans did it in the 1940s, and surely we could figure it out today.

Last, if we as a society truly support the development of renewable sources such as windmills and solar cells, they could replace much of the fossil fuels used today in the electric grid system. With that development, plus judicious conservation, we would have a lot of energy left over for the transportation sector, the part of the economy that is using up the oil and making us worry about hydrogen in the first place.

The Author

Matthew L. Wald is a reporter at the New York Times, *where he has been covering energy since 1979. He has written about oil refining; coal mining; electricity production from coal, natural gas, uranium, wind and solar energy; electric and hybrid automobiles; and air pollution from energy use. His current assignment is in Washington, D.C., where he also writes about transportation safety and other technical topics.*

It may be a few more years until engineers get a new fuel cell right. But what do we do in the meantime? How can we power our current cars more efficiently in the next few years? The short-term solution might come not in another fuel, but rather in another type of engine, as Steven Ashley suggests in the following article. Could the homogeneous charge compression ignition (HCCI) engine be that engine? Researchers say the HCCI engine has the potential to offer high efficiency and low emissions before the fuel cell is perfected, but a number of hurdles must be overcome before this engine solution becomes a reality. —SW

"A Low-Pollution Engine Solution"
by **Steven Ashley**
Scientific American, **June 2001**

Anyone who has driven a car, truck or motorcycle that is at least 20 years old is probably familiar with what engineers call after-run, an annoying and now rare condition in which an engine keeps turning over for a few seconds after the ignition is off. But today the fundamental fuel-burning process that causes after-run is firing the interest of the automotive industry. Known as homogeneous-charge compression-ignition combustion, or HCCI, the process could provide the basis for a new class of low-emission, high-mileage power plants. Many combustion engineers believe that HCCI-based piston engines will be able to deliver the good fuel economy of diesel engines without the diesel's high emissions of nitrogen oxides and soot.

Faced with increasingly stringent governmental pollution standards as well as the realization that practical and affordable fuel cell technology (in large production volumes) is still many years away, researchers at the world's major automakers and diesel-engine manufacturers are working to determine whether HCCI technology will be technically and economically feasible. If so, power plants based on this new combustion mode might serve as a potential bridge technology between today's high-emission diesel- and gasoline-fueled piston engines and tomorrow's ultraclean fuel cell power trains.

Standing-room-only attendance at the technical sessions on HCCI combustion at the recent Society of Automotive Engineers (SAE) 2001 World Congress in Detroit is one strong indication that the homogeneous-charge compression-ignition engine could be the next big thing in the car industry. Another is the marked rise in the numbers of technical papers written on the topic, says Dennis Assanis, professor of mechanical engineering at the University of Michigan at Ann Arbor and director of the university's Automotive Research Center. "Since 1995, when only a few HCCI papers were published, we've seen what seems to be an exponential increase," he reports.

Yet another sign of HCCI's newfound status is growing research support from the U.S. Department of Energy, which began funding its study in 1997. The Partnership for a New Generation of Vehicles, an R&D consortium involving government, industry and university scientists and engineers devoted to advanced automotive technology, has established a $3-million, four-year academic research program on the novel combustion process. At the same time, industry and academic researchers in the field have prepared a report to the U.S. Congress about the technology. Interest is also great in Japan, where engineers who pioneered the exploitation of HCCI call it active thermo-atmosphere combustion, and in Europe, where it is known as controlled auto-ignition.

Burning Lean and Clean

HCCI can be thought of as a crossbreed technology combining attractive aspects of both conventional gasoline and diesel engines to achieve good fuel economy and near-zero exhaust emissions. Roughly speaking, internal-combustion engines fall into four categories, defined by the degree of mixing in the charge of fuel and air in the cylinder and by how this charge is ignited. The familiar gasoline engine, in which a premixed, thoroughly commingled fuel-air charge is set aflame by a spark plug, falls into the spark-ignited, homogeneous-mixture classification. The diesel engine is an example of the compression-ignition, heterogeneous-mixture type: fuel is sprayed into the cylinder during the piston's compression stroke, and turbulent flow partially mixes it with air until the rising temperature induces burning. The gasoline direct-injection engine, in which injected fuel partially mixes with air until set alight by a spark, is considered a spark-ignited, heterogeneous engine. As its name indicates, the homogeneous-charge compression-ignition engine is a fourth type: it uses a thoroughly premixed charge of fuel and air that is compressed by a piston until it self-ignites.

Because the amount of burning fuel is low in comparison to the volume of air inside an HCCI engine, the combustion temperatures stay relatively low. That means the engine produces only small quantities of nitrogen oxide and dioxide (collectively, NO_x). Also,

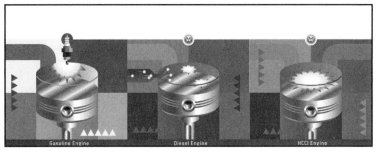

Crossbreed concept: The homogeneous-charge compression-ignition (HCCI) engine can be considered a hybrid of the spark-ignition or gasoline engine and the compression-ignition or diesel engine. Gasoline engines use a premixed or homogeneous fuel-air charge that is placed in the cylinder and then ignited by a spark plug, causing a hot flame front to sweep through the charge. In diesel engines, fuel is injected into the cylinder during the piston's compression stroke, where it partially mixes with the air (producing a heterogeneous mixture) until the rising temperature induces self-ignition.

An HCCI power plant would combine aspects of both—the premixed fuel-air charge of the gasoline engine and the pressure-heated auto-ignition of the diesel—to produce a low-temperature, even-burning combustion process that yields good fuel efficiency as well as low emissions of nitrogen oxides and soot in the exhaust.

because the charge is well mixed and does not contain excess fuel, the combustion generates only small amounts of sooty particulates. Engine efficiencies are high because the HCCI combustion process allows the use of high, diesel-like compression ratios (generating more power per unit of fuel burned) and because, like diesels, HCCI engines can meet load demands without the use of intake throttling, thus eliminating so-called breathing losses. In addition, if properly engineered, these power plants could burn nearly any available hydrocarbon fuel or even hydrogen.

Automotive engineers and combustion researchers are pursuing this alternative form of the internal-combustion engine because current propulsion configurations are not likely to meet upcoming environmental regulations that will place severe limits on exhaust containing greenhouse gases—mostly carbon dioxide—and other pollutants, including NO_x, particulates, carbon monoxide and unburned hydrocarbons. The gasoline engine runs too hot and is too fuel-inefficient to make the grade. Poor fuel economy translates into excessive production of carbon dioxide, whereas high-temperature combustion yields too much NO_x. In contrast, the fuel-efficient diesel engine generates too much NO_x and particulate emissions to satisfy soon-to-be-imposed pollution standards. Although catalytic after-treatment systems offer hope that exhaust emissions from these conventional power plants can be cleaned up after the fact, there is no surety that this can be accomplished affordably. Direct-injection gasoline engines offer better fuel economy, but their NO_x and hydrocarbon emission levels are not much lower than their conventional gasoline counterparts. As such, they would still require the use of sophisticated exhaust after-treatment systems, which, in turn, need new grades of low-sulfur gasoline to avoid poisoning their catalysts.

Existing alternative propulsion technologies seem to provide little or no respite in the search for an environmentally and economically sound personal transportation technology for the near-term future. Because of the energy storage limitations of electro-chemical batteries, electric cars now offer insufficient driving range, at best about 160 miles. The electric car's overall environmental fitness is, moreover, dependent on the cleanliness of the method employed to generate electric power. Widespread use of coal-burning power plants, for example, reduces the electric car's total system cleanliness substantially. Today's hybrid electric vehicles, which combine downsized internal-combustion engines with batteries and electric motors, produce less pollution than current cars and trucks, but auto companies must subsidize their price tags by as much as $10,000 apiece to make them cost-competitive with conventional vehicles. As a result, automotive engineers are searching for ways to improve the internal-combustion engine so that it can carry the industry through the forthcoming transition to ultraclean, next-generation propulsion systems.

Taking the Load

HCCI combustion has been studied by many inventors and engineers under many different guises during the past century. But according to Paul Najt, spark-ignition-engine group manager at the General Motors Research and Development Center in Warren, Mich., the modern investigation of this unique combustion mode actually began in the late 1970s. At that time, a research team led by Shigeru Onishi of Nippon Clean Engine Company in Japan reported that it had been studying what members called active thermo-atmosphere combustion in two-stroke engines. "Rather than avoid this natural mode of combustion, Onishi said: 'Let's try to exploit it,'" says Najt, who was an engineering school graduate student in the early 1980s. He and his fellow students took up the challenge but soon found that the engine controls of the day could not manage the difficult task of controlling the auto-ignition process as engine speeds and loads were varied. Unfortunately, that problem remains unsolved.

"The HCCI process really works well in the laboratory on a dynamometer when all the engine components are in thermal equilibrium," explains Thomas Asmus, senior research executive at DaimlerChrysler Liberty and Technical Affairs in Rochester Hills, Mich. "But when you add a load and try to make the engine do work, as it would in a vehicle, it just tends to slow down and stop completely. If you add more fuel so it can handle the increased load, it tends to start knocking very seriously." Nearly all HCCI experts mention how an engine running in HCCI mode can easily "run away on you," producing a tremendous pounding noise that will eventually destroy the engine hardware.

The problem is twofold, Asmus says. First, HCCI combustion occurs extremely quickly. Once the temperature in the engine cylinder is sufficiently high, the premixed fuel-air mixture ignites all at once. "For use in a practical engine, we need the combustion to have a smoother, more extended heat-release profile," he explains. For maximum efficiency, designers prefer for the ignition process to begin at 10 to 15 degrees of crank angle before the piston reaches top dead center and then the remainder to continue afterward. If the burn starts too early, the hot gas is exposed to the cylinder walls for too long and heat is lost, cutting efficiency. If it starts too late, the hot combustion gases do not undergo full expansion and therefore do not impart maximum work to the piston.

The second problem with HCCI, Asmus says, revolves around the fact that "there's no triggering event, like a spark or fuel injection, which are the handles we use for controlling the timing of the burn event" in conventional engines. To keep the process under control as speed and load changes occur (operating conditions that engineers call transients), the engine has to make very rapid adjustments from one cycle to the next. Currently no one knows exactly how to accomplish that reliably and affordably. "With HCCI," he points out, "it's not clear what will serve as a strong, robust lever for phasing the burn."

Najt concurs: "The benefits of HCCI are clear; the difficulty is in controlling HCCI combustion. Right now it's a question of technology execution. All kinds of control concepts that 20 years ago seemed a bit over the edge are being considered. It may be that, relative to fuel cell technology, these kinds of technologies and the extra cost to implement them don't seem as much of a stretch."

These still unproved engine-control technologies are manifold. They include variable-valve actuation, in

which hot residuals—embers from the previous burn—
are inducted into the cylinder to control the phasing of
the next burn cycle. Variable-valve-timing systems are
based on "camless valve trains" operated by electromagnetic, electrohydraulic or piezoelectric actuators
rather than mechanical cams. To get the needed cycle-
to-cycle response-rate resolution, however, the valves
have to move extremely rapidly, and that kind of
operation is difficult to keep up over the lifetime of
an engine.

Another possibility, Dennis Assanis says, is to use
variable-compression-ratio systems, which involve
changing the volume of the combustion chamber, and
so the compression ratio, on the fly. This effect can be
accomplished by opening and closing engine valves at
the appropriate time or by installing pistons that alter
their height in accordion fashion in reaction to pressure
changes, a radical concept that is under investigation
at the University of Michigan in cooperation with Ford
Motor Company and Federal Mogul Corporation.

Yet another approach being looked at by many
researchers is to add some inhomogeneity (variation in
local density and temperature) into the fuel-air mixture
to extend the duration of the burn. Of course, "that's
like playing with the devil," Assanis notes. "You're
giving up some homogeneity [thus boosting pollutant
output] to get a smoother heat release."

"The problem with these advanced concepts,"
Najt says, "is that they introduce a whole series of
mechanical-complexity and cost issues. The use of

two unproved technologies often squares the difficulty of the original problem. And the cost of integrating them into a viable package may be too great."

Handling High Loads and Hybrids

Even if these obstacles are surmounted, another overall concern must be addressed. Because the fuel-air mixture has to be lean (a low fuel fraction in relation to the volume of air) to obtain the emissions benefits, HCCI is suitable only for light and medium loads and speeds. To handle higher loads and speeds, more fuel needs to be added to the mixture, but doing so would raise combustion temperatures and eliminate much of the environmental benefit. Therefore, HCCI combustion would probably be used in what engineers call dual-mode engines. At high engine loads, the system would switch from auto-igniting HCCI mode to spark ignition (in gasoline-fueled engines) or to standard fuel injection (in diesel engines).

Najt notes that the most straightforward application of HCCI would probably be in a fuel-efficient hybrid-electric vehicle, which combines an internal-combustion engine, an electric motor and a battery. When used in a hybrid configuration, the internal-combustion engine, whether it is of the HCCI type or not, operates in a smaller speed and load range. As this suits clean-burning HCCI technology, this may turn out to be a perfect match for the hybrid-electric configuration. "Yet it's not clear that HCCI will end up as the optimal engine for hybrids, because even hybrids run through a fairly extensive speed and load range, so the engine must follow any increased load demands," he comments. This is the case because the energy storage capacity of today's batteries is not large enough to provide all the extra power for acceleration and hill climbing when it is needed.

The technical hurdles that must still be overcome have obviously done nothing to suppress enthusiasm for HCCI within much of the engineering community. Some observers wonder, however, whether it will really prove to be the long-sought-after solution to the environmental/economic quandary. Every few years the auto industry focuses eagerly on a particular engine technology as the next big thing that might do the trick, Najt says. Less optimistic experts attending the recent SAE sessions called HCCI the latest boutique engine.

"In the mid-1980s it was the two-stroke engine, which didn't pan out," Najt explains. "A couple of years ago it was the gasoline direct-injection engine, which, although it has been relatively successful, doesn't seem to be a panacea."

Many engine researchers expect that HCCI-based power plants will be the first automotive engines designed "from the inside out." In other words, using advanced computational modeling techniques, engineers will be able to explore the chemical kinetics of fuel-oxidation and fluid-mechanics phenomena associated with mixing and burning that control HCCI before they settle on an engine design. Nevertheless, a lot of good old experimental work with test engines will be needed before a practical, affordable engine can be developed.

"Clearly, it's too early to tell whether HCCI will prove to be successful," Najt concludes. "It's a high-risk technology." Still, most engineers agree that it is worth exploring while we're waiting for something cleaner to come along.

The Author

Steven Ashley is a staff editor and writer.

Web Sites

Due to the changing nature of Internet links, the Rosen Publishing Group, Inc., has developed an online list of Web sites related to the subject of this book. This site is updated regularly. Please use this link to access the list:

http://www.rosenlinks.com/saca/poll

For Further Reading

Anderson, Bob, and Joanne Buggey. *Pollution: Examining Cause and Effect Relationships*. San Diego, CA: Greenhaven Press, 1992.

Bowker, Michael. *Fatal Deception: How Big Business Is Still Killing Us with Asbestos*. New York, NY: Rodale Books, 2003.

Bryan, Nichol. Exxon Valdez: *Oil Spill*. New York, NY: World Almanac Library, 2003.

Collinson, Alan. *Pollution*. New York, NY: New Discovery Books, 1992.

Dolan, Edward F. *Our Poisoned Waters*. New York, NY: Dutton Books, 1997.

Gay, Kathlyn. *Pollution and the Powerless: The Environmental Justice Movement*. London, England: Franklin Watts, 1995.

Haley, James, ed. *Pollution* (Current Controversies). San Diego, CA: Greenhaven Press, 2002.

Kidd, J. S., and Renee A. Kidd. *Into Thin Air: The Problem of Air Pollution*. New York, NY: Facts on File, 1998.

Meharg, Andrew. *Venomous Earth: How Arsenic Caused the World's Worst Mass Poisoning*. New York, NY: Macmillan, 2005.

Newton, David E. *Taking a Stand Against Environmental Pollution*. London, England: Franklin Watts, 1990.

Roleff, Tamara L. *Pollution: Opposing Viewpoints*. San Diego, CA: Greenhaven Press, 2000.

Snodgrass, Mary Ellen, Jody Adams, and Janet Wolanin. *Environmental Awareness: Acid Rain*. Minneapolis, MN: Bancroft-Sage Publishing, 1991.

Snodgrass, Mary Ellen, Marjorie L. Oelerich, Jody Adams, and Janet Wolanin. *Environmental Awareness: Water Pollution*. Minneapolis, MN: Bancroft-Sage Publishing, 1991.

Bibliography

Airhart, Marc. "Cleaning Up After War." *Scientific American*, October 2003, pp. 44–45.

Alleman, James E., and Brooke T. Mossman. "Asbestos Revisited." *Scientific American*, July 1997, pp. 70–75.

American Cancer Society. "How Many Women Get Breast Cancer?" January 1, 2005. Retrieved June 23, 2005 (http://www.cancer.org/docroot/CRI/content/CRI_2_2_1X_How_many_people_get_breast_cancer_5.asp?sitearea =).

Angelina, Michael E., and Jennifer L. Biggs. "Analyzing Reserves: Devil Is in the Details: As Scrutiny, Case Filings Rise, Insurers Must Consider a Host of Factors." *National Underwriter Property & Casualty-Risk & Benefits Management*, June 28, 2004, pp. 18–20.

Ashley, Steven. "A Low-Pollution Engine Solution." *Scientific American*, June 2001, pp. 90–95.

Bagla, Pallava. "Arsenic-Laced Well Water Poisoning Bangladeshis." *National Geographic News*, June 5, 2003. Retrieved June 28, 2005 (http://news.nationalgeographic.com/news/2003/06/0605_030605_arsenicwater.html).

BBC News. "Historic Smog Death Toll Rises." December 5, 2002. Retrieved July 12, 2005 (http://news.bbc.co.uk/1/hi/health/2545747.stm).

Béland, Pierre. "The Beluga Whales of the St. Lawrence River." *Scientific American*, May 1996, pp. 74–81.

Bhopal Information Center. "Chronology." October 2004. Retrieved July 12, 2005 (http://www.bhopal.com/chrono.htm).

Blaustein, Andrew R., and Pieter T. J. Johnson. "Explaining Frog Deformities." *Scientific American*, February 2003, pp. 60–65.

Canada Fisheries and Oceans. "Canada's Species at Risk Act." July 20, 2004. Retrieved July 6, 2005 (http://www.dfo-mpo.gc.ca/species-especes/species/species_belugaStLawrence_e.asp).

Chen, David. "GM's Strategy: Advanced Propulsion Technologies." General Motors. Retrieved July 10, 2005 (http://www.iea.org/textbase/work/2004/shanghai/Chen.PDF).

Chowdhury, A. Mushtaque R. "Arsenic Crisis in Bangladesh." *Scientific American*, August 2004, pp. 86–91.

CNN.com. "Despite Toxic History, Residents Return to Love Canal." August 7, 1998. Retrieved July 12, 2005 (http://www.cnn.com/US/9808/07/love.canal/).

CNN.com. "Honda Leases First Fuel Cell Car in U.S." July 6, 2005. Retrieved July 10, 2005 (http://www.cnn.com/2005/TECH/07/06/spark.car.reut/).

Davis, Devra Lee, and H. Leon Bradlow. "Can Environmental Estrogens Cause Breast Cancer?" *Scientific American*, October 1995, pp. 166–170.

Dr. Susan Love Foundation. "Environmental Estrogens and Breast Cancer: The Latest." March 10, 2000.

Retrieved June 23, 2005 (http://www.susanlovemd. org/community/flashes/hotflash000310.htm).

"Efforts to Stop Pollution." *Monkeyshines on America: U.S. Environments*, August 2000, p. 23.

"Engine Shows Diesel Efficiency Without the Emissions." *Science & Technology*, April 2004. Retrieved July 10, 2005 (http://www.llnl.gov/str/ April04/Aceves.html).

Environmental Protection Agency. "Review of the National Ambient Air Quality Standards for Particulate Matter: Policy Assessment of Scientific and Technical Information." June 2005. Retrieved July 10, 2005 (http://www.epa.gov/ttn/naaqs/ standards/pm/data/pmstaffpaper_20050630.pdf).

"EPA Reports Continued Improvements in Ambient Air Quality." *Air Pollution Consultant*, January 2003, pp. 1–5.

European Commission. "Clean Urban Transport." Retrieved July 10, 2005 (http://europa.eu.int/comm/ energy_transport/en/cut_en.html).

"Europe Opens Hydrogen Fuel Testing Center." *Environment News Service*, July 8, 2005. Retrieved July 10, 2005 (http://www.ens-newswire.com/ens/ jul2005/2005-07-08-01.asp).

Fonda, Daren. "After the Spill: Ten Years Later, Alaska's Wilderness Still Struggles to Heal." *Life*, April 1, 1999, p. 103.

Greenberg, Karl. "Green Is Good: From Hybrid Cars to Hydrogen Fuel Cells, Automakers Are Ushering in New Technologies for a Greener Market." *Brandweek*, January 3, 2005, pp. 16–20.

Hedin, Lars O., and Gene E. Likens. "Atmospheric Dust and Acid Rain." *Scientific American,* December 1996, pp. 88–92.

Henson, Rosemarie, L. Medina, S. St. Clair, D. Blanke, L. Downs, and J. Jordan. "Clean Indoor Air: Where, Why, and How." *Journal of Law, Medicine & Ethics,* Fall 2002, pp. S75–86.

Herring, David. "Terra Turns Five." February 28, 2005. Retrieved July 10, 2005 (http://earthobservatory. nasa.gov/Study/Terra/).

"It's Time to Put the *Valdez* Behind Us." *Business Week,* March 29, 1999, p. 90.

King, Michael D., and David D. Herring. "Monitoring Earth's Vital Signs." *Scientific American,* April 2000, pp. 92–97.

Krajick, Kevin. "Long-Term Data Show Lingering Effects from Acid Rain." *Science,* April 13, 2001, p. 195.

Mitra, A. K., F. S. Faruque, and Amanda Avis. "Breast Cancer and Environmental Risks: Where Is the Link?" *Journal of Environmental Health,* March 2004, pp. 24–32.

Monastersky, Richard. "Ancient Metal Mines Sullied Global Skies." *Science News,* April 13, 1996, pp. 230–231.

"More Stringent Standards for Particulates Recommended by EPA Staff to Protect Health." *BNA Daily Environment Report,* July 5, 2005. Retrieved July 10, 2005 (http://ehscenter.bna.com/ pic2/ehs.nsf/id/BNAP-6DZE2Z?OpenDocument).

National Aeronautics and Space Administration. "TERRA: The EOS Flagship." April 15, 2005. Retrieved July 10, 2005 (http://terra.nasa.gov/).

National Cancer Institute. "Asbestos Exposure: Questions and Answers." Last updated August 29, 2003. Retrieved July 5, 2005 (http://cis.nci.nih.gov/fact/3_21.htm).

Nature Canada. "Endangered Species: St. Lawrence River Beluga Whale." Retrieved July 6, 2005 (http://www.cnf.ca/species/critters/beluga.html).

New York State Department of Health. "A Guide to the New York State Clean Indoor Air Act." July 24, 2003. Retrieved June 23, 2005 (http://www.health.state.ny.us/nysdoh/clean_indoor_air_act/general.htm).

Nixon, Scott W. "Enriching the Sea to Death." *Scientific American Presents: The Oceans*, Fall 1998, pp. 48–53.

Okey, Thomas. "Lost Eden." *E*, May 2000, p. 34.

Ott, Wayne R., and John W. Roberts. "Everyday Exposure to Toxic Pollutants." *Scientific American*, February 1998, pp. 86–91.

Oweis, Khaled Yacoub. "Postwar Iraq Paying Heavy Environmental Price." Reuters. June 2, 2005. Retrieved June 20, 2005 (http://www.commondreams.org/headlines05/0602-21.htm).

Pelley, Janet. "Can Nutrient Loads Predict Marine Water Quality?" *Environmental Science and Technology*, January 19, 2005. Retrieved June 20, 2005 (http://pubs.acs.org/subscribe/journals/esthag-w/2005/jan/science/jp_nutrient.html#).

"Pollution." *Microsoft Encarta Online Encyclopedia.* Retrieved July 12, 2005 (http://encarta.msn.com/encyclopedia_761570933/Pollution.html).

Raloff, Janet. "Air Sickness: How Microscopic Dust Particles Cause Subtle but Serious Harm." *ScienceNews Online,* August 2, 2003. Retrieved July 10, 2005 (http://www.sciencenews.org/articles/20030802/bob8.asp).

Robb, Matthew. "Indoor Air Quality Is a Top Health Risk." *Washington Post,* April 9, 2005, p. F01.

Senkowsky, Sonya. "The Oil and the Otter." *Scientific American,* May 2004, pp. 30–31.

Sherman, Don. "The Internal Combustion Engine's Last Hurrah: Homogeneous-Charge Compression-Ignition May Be the Answer." *Automotive Industries,* December 2004, pp. 44–46.

The Simpsons.com Episode Guide. Retrieved July 5, 2005 (http://www.thesimpsons.com/episode_guide/).

Stix, Gary. "Where the Bodies Lie." *Scientific American,* June 1998, pp. 30–32.

United Nations. "History of the United Nations and Chernobyl." Retrieved July 12, 2005 (http://www.un.org/ha/chernobyl/).

United Nations Environment Program. "Environment in Iraq: UNEP Progress Report." October 20, 2003. Retrieved June 20, 2005 (http://postconflict.unep.ch/publications/Iraq_PR.pdf).

U.S. Department of Agriculture. "Agricultural Phosphorous and Eutrophication, 2nd Edition."

Last updated September 2003. Retrieved June 20, 2005 (http://www.ars.usda.gov/is/np/Phos&Eutro2/agphoseutro2ed.pdf).

U.S. Department of Energy. "The Hydrogen Future." Retrieved July 10, 2005 (http://www.eere.energy.gov/hydrogenandfuelcells/future/economy.html).

U.S. Environmental Protection Agency. "Acid Rain." January 3, 2005. Retrieved June 20, 2005 (http://www.epa.gov/airmarkets/acidrain/).

U.S. Environmental Protection Agency. "Arsenic in Drinking Water." Retrieved June 28, 2005 (http://www.epa.gov/safewater/arsenic.html).

U.S. Environmental Protection Agency. "Clean Air Interstate Rule." March 10, 2005. Retrieved June 20, 2005 (http://www.epa.gov/interstateairquality/).

U.S. Environmental Protection Agency. "Ecoregional Nutrient Criteria: Fact Sheet." Last updated October 2002. Retrieved June 20, 2005. (http://www.epa.gov/waterscience/criteria/nutrient/ecoregions/jan03frnfs.pdf).

Vince, Gaia. "Earth's Ozone Depletion Is Finally Slowing." NewScientist.com. July 30, 2003. Retrieved July 12, 2005. (http://www.newscientist.com/article.ns?id = dn4010).

Wald, Matthew L. "Questions About a Hydrogen Economy." *Scientific American*, May 2004, pp. 66–73.

Warfel, William. "The Rocky Road to Asbestos Litigation Reform." *Risk Management*, November 2004, pp. 20–24.

Woellert, Lorraine. "The Asbestos Mess: There Is a Way Out." *Business Week*, April 18, 2005, p. 40.

World Health Organization. "Arsenic in Drinking Water." Fact Sheet No. 210, May 2001. Retrieved June 28, 2005 (http://www.who.int/mediacentre/factsheets/fs210/en/).

World Health Organization. "Researchers Warn of Impending Disaster from Mass Arsenic Poisoning." Press release, September 8, 2000. Retrieved June 28, 2005 (http://www.who.int/inf-pr-2000/en/pr2000-55.html).

Index

About the Editor

Stephanie Watson is a writer specializing in consumer health and science. She has written and contributed to more than a dozen works, including *The Mechanisms of Genetics: An Anthology of Current Thought*, *Science and Its Times*, *World of Genetics*, *Science in Dispute*, and *The Endocrine System*. Ms. Watson lives and works in Atlanta, Georgia.

Illustration Credits

Cover Getty Images; pp. 14–15, 23, 147 Roberto Osti; pp. 18, 55, 59 Jennifer C. Christiansen; pp. 35, 39, 143, 161, 163–164 (Terra boxes), 166–168 (Terra icons) Laurie Grace; pp. 69, 83, 170, 175 Johnny Johnson; p. 74 Tomo Narashima; p. 92 Lucy Reading and Jana Brenning; pp. 100, 187, 190 Lucy Reading; p. 132 David Fierstein; pp. 160, 163–164 (Terra icons), 167–168 (Terra boxes) George Retseck; pp. 193, 195 Slim Films; p. 201 Jose Cruz.

Series Designer: Tahara Anderson
Series Editor: Kathy Kuhtz Campbell